Oven Baked

DUMONT monte

Over 120 delicious recipes

Oven Baked

Conny Strauß

DUMONT
monte

Notes

Beef: Always buy top quality beef from a reliable butcher. Ask the origin of the beef and the abattoir from which it comes.

Eggs: Unless otherwise stated, the recipes refer to standard or medium-sized eggs.

Milk: Unless otherwise stated, the recipes refer to full-cream milk (at least 3.5% fat).

Poultry: Poultry should always be properly cooked all the way through. This can be checked by pricking the flesh with a fork. Check the leg, which takes longest to cook. If the juices run red or pink, it means that the poultry is not sufficiently cooked and must be cooked longer. If the juices are clear, the poultry is cooked.

Nuts: Some recipes in this book contain nuts or oil made from nuts. People who suffer from nut allergies or who are in general prone to allergies should not eat these dishes.

Herbs: Unless otherwise stated, fresh herbs should always be used for the recipes in this book. If fresh herbs cannot be found, they may be replaced with half the quantity of dried herbs.

The times and temperatures given for the recipes refer to ordinary (convection) ovens. If a fan oven is used, the maker's instructions should be followed.

Contents

Introduction

Casseroles, gratins and soufflés are undoubtedly among the among the most popular dishes with both gourmets and cooks. These delicious, irresistibly fragrant oven-baked dishes are to be found in many parts of the world, from Italy and France, to Mexico and Turkey.

Main course or dessert?

Whether the dish is a satisfying main meal or a light dessert, these popular oven dishes with their delicious crust or topping are simple to put together. Most of the work is done at the start. Once the dish has been prepared it can confidently be left unattended in the oven for the duration of the cooking time while the cook attends to other things, whether it be clearing the kitchen or simply relaxing with the family and any guests.

Keep an eye on freshness

With baked dishes as with all recipes, the quality of the ingredients used is of fundamental importance. so where possible only fresh vegetables or fruit should be used. If stored too long, so that they become somewhat wilted, vegetables and fruit lose the best of their flavour, and they will only contain a proportion of the vitamins they would have had at the time they were harvested. The meat specified in the list of ingredients should be bought from a reliable butcher who enjoys the confidence of his customers, and who knows the source from which his beef, pork and lamb comes.

Caution with eggs!

Eggs play an essential role in the making of many gratins and all soufflés, so their quality too is important. The best ones to use are fresh eggs from free-range chickens. Eggs from non-battery chickens that are kept on the ground in a confined area are not necessarily eggs from healthy chickens. This method of egg production means that, instead of being limited to a cage, the chickens can also wander around on the ground inside the chicken coop. But the problem is that since the animals are crowded into a relatively small area, they often have to receive continuous medication to prevent them catching infectious diseases from each other.

Which cheeses are best for baking?

Many oven dishes acquire their beautiful crust from the cheese with which they are baked. Various kinds of hard and medium-hard cheese are particularly suitable for this, including Emmental, Gouda, Parmesan, mountain cheese, as well as the stronger-tasting Gruyère or Appenzell. In some cases cream cheese and mozzarella are also used. The latter admittedly has little flavour of its own, but it melts beautifully with an elastic quality and forms a superb brown crust.

For a stronger cheese flavour, the cheeses suggested in the recipes may always be replaced with Gruyère or Appenzell. A more piquant taste is given by blue cheeses such as Roquefort, Gorgonzola and Stilton,

It is important that all the other ingredients and the sauce should be sufficiently moist so that the dish does not become not too dry.

Solid vegetables and meat require a longer cooking time, and these are normally pre-cooked before the dish is put in the oven. They are then baked in the oven at a higher temperatures.

The same principle applies to dishes that make use of left-overs, such as vegetables, noodles or potatoes, since these too are pre-cooked. In this case the cooking temperature must be high so that a protective crust forms quickly over the surface of the casserole.

As is always the case, there are exceptions to every rule. The celebrated French potato gratin dishes are cooked with raw potatoes rather than pre-cooked ones. The dish is cooked for a relatively long time at a medium heat.

Soufflé, gratin or casserole?

What distinguishes the terms soufflé, gratin and casserole? A "soufflé" is relatively easy to describe, being any dish that expands during cooking, usually above the level of the mould or dish in which it is cooked. This phenomenon is caused by the expansion of the air in stiffly-beaten egg whites when heated in the oven. A soufflé, then, will invariably contain beaten egg whites.

A "gratin" is a dish that acquires a golden brown top by being cooked in the oven. Often the crust will consist of cheese or breadcrumbs, and it will form a protective layer when formed so that the contents of the dish remain moist.

or milder ones such as Bleu d'Auvergne and Mascarpone-Gorgonzola.

In fact the choice of cheese is up to the cook, the only requirement being that it should always be freshly grated since this invariably tastes better and more full of flavour.

Pre-cooked or raw ingredients

There are two methods of preparing oven-baked dishes: using pre-cooked ingredients or raw ones. Fish and soft or thinly-sliced vegetables cook very quickly done, so they can be used raw and stacked roughly in layers in the dish, which is then baked at medium heat until the dish is done.

The word "casserole" simply describes any dish that is baked in the oven and contained in a casserole.

Casserole or baked dishes

Dishes baked in casseroles are normally served as main dish, because a typical characteristic is their rich composition. Almost any ingredients can be cooked in this way, including bread, noodles, rice, potatoes, vegetables or meat. Left-over food can also easily be used in preparing them without the quality suffering from it – quite the opposite, in fact: a casserole prepared with left-overs can be extremely delicious. It is only important that all the ingredients should have the same cooking time.

Any items that require a longer cooking time than the rest must be pre-cooked or ready-cooked before they are added to the casserole dish. The whole dish is usually held together with a mixture of egg and milk and it is also often cooked with cheese.

The same cooking principles apply whether the ingredients are savoury or sweet. Sweet baked dishes are based on somewhat lighter ingredients and sometimes use a sponge mixture.

As a rule, all dished baked in casseroles can be made in advance. Many can be prepared and put in the cooking dish or mould well before any guests arrive. Only the egg and milk mixture should be omitted until just before the dish is about to be cooked, so that the ingredients do not have time absorb all the liquid.

Casseroles are usually bakes on the middle or lower shelf of the oven.

Gratins

Almost any dish can be baked as a gratin: starters (appetizers) and main dishes, as well as side dishes and puddings. Gratins typically have a shorter cooking time at a higher temperature than casserole baked dishes. The ingredients are nearly always pre-cooked to some extent and then finished in a light sauce in the oven. As usual, there are exceptions to this principle.

Like dishes baked in casseroles, gratins can also be prepared several hours before the meal. Again, the sauce should be added only just before the dish is put in the oven. It should not be allowed to cool too much before being poured or it may become too solid and thick. Often the cheese is grated and added to the top of the dish only half-way through the cooking time. A few flakes of butter on top will round off the whole dish beautifully.

Gratins are cooked on the middle or upper shelf of the pre-heated oven so that the delicious crust can develop.

Soufflés

While casseroles and gratins dishes have the reputation of being dishes even beginners can prepare with ease, soufflés are widely regarded as being difficult. But in fact the difficulty is exaggerated, as anyone who has made one of these exquisitely airy confections will confirm. It is important to follow the recipe instructions exactly, but if this is done nothing should actually fail. If the worst happens and the soufflé collapses, it is not the end of the world. The texture will be different but the taste will still be just as delicious.

The basic recipe consists of making a bechamel sauce, into which the respective ingredients are mixed and bound with egg yolks. Independently, the egg whites are beaten to stiff peaks and the other mixture is then gently folded into them, so that the entire mass loses as little volume as possible. The best way to do this is to start by incorporating the mixture into one-third of the beaten egg white with a whisk, then fold in the rest gently with a wooden spatula.

A heatproof round soufflé dish large enough for the mixture to fill it only two-thirds full is needed, so that the soufflé has plenty of room to rise with the effect of the heat. It is also best to grease the base only of the soufflé dish; otherwise the delicate mass of the soufflé might slip back with the melting of the butter on the sides.

Soufflés are baked on the lowest shelf in the oven. The oven door should not under any account be opened during the first three-quarters of the cooking time, or the soufflé will collapse. In fact it is safest to wait until the cooking is complete.

Incidentally, it is also possible to make a soufflé using the principle of the bain marie or double boiler. The escaping steam makes the soufflé rise particularly well. A pan at least 1 cm/⅜ in larger all round than the soufflé dish is needed. It is filled with enough water to come about 5 cm/2 in up the side of the soufflé dish. The whole is put in the pre-heated oven and as cooked described in the recipe method. If the surface of the souffle is not browned enough at the end of the cooking time, it may be carefully removed from the pan of water and put back in the oven for about 5 or 10 minutes. In this way the surface will end up with a beautiful brown crust.

The right dish and some useful gadgets

The dish in which a baked dish is prepared and cooked is a entirely a matter of choice for the cook.

It may be a container made of earthenware, porcelain china or glass, or a stainless steel or cast iron cooking pot. The only requirement is that it should be fireproof.

In the case of gratin dishes, these are made of ceramics or ovenproof glass; they tend to be relatively large and shallow, so that the area of the crust is as large as possible.

For soufflés, the material used for the dish is not crucial. Porcelain, glazed earthenware or glass are equally suitable.

The shape of the dish is preferably round and tall so that the souffle can rise evenly in all its magnificence and not overflow.

Whatever the kind of dish, the majority of the work takes place in the preparation of the ingredients in the first place. Here then are some useful kitchen gadget that can help in the process preparation process.

For slicing, a mandoline is extremely useful. It enables potatoes to be cut into really thin disks, for example.

For the preparation of various vegetables, a raw vegetable grater is often useful.

A cheese grater is virtually an essential tool, since cheese is needed for almost every casserole, and freshly grated cheese tastes much better than that bought already grated.

Cooking times and the right temperature

All ovens are different and at the same setting they may reach different temperatures. The cooking times stated with the recipes are therefore not definitive. The cook will quickly find out if a dish needs five minutes more or less in the oven used. Incidentally, the oven can normally be turned off about ten min-

utes before the end of the cooking time. The heat will still be enough to finish cooking the casserole, and doing so saves energy.

The cooking temperatures given in the recipes are suitable for most ovens. The temperature of fan ovens may be a little lower to achieve the same result.

Cooking in the microwave

In principle, all dishes for baking in the oven can also be prepared in the microwave. But since gratins and soufflés should form a beautiful golden brown crust, a problem is that an ordinary microwave will not achieve this.

A combination microwave with grill is therefore recommended. This has traditional heating elements in the top of the oven in addition to the heat provided by the microwave energy.

All combination microwaves have a choice of power levels. The highest ranges from 600 to 800 watts and this is used for reheating and fast cooking of vegetables, for instance. Lower temperatures are used for dishes that require a longer cooking time, and lower still for sensitive dishes such as egg and other sauces.

The manufacturer's instructions should be followed. The various power levels are an advantage for baked dishes since they enable the cooking time to be long enough for the grill to brown the topping.

An important consideration when cooking in the microwave is that all ingredients must have the same cooking time. Any ingredients requiring a longer time than the other components of the dish should be pre-cooked to allow for this.

Metal containers must never be used in a microwave, and plastic ones must be avoided if the grill is used. Dishes made from glass, porcelain or glazed earthenware are ideal since they can be used in all circumstances. The only point to watch is that they have no metallic glaze or decoration. Finally, there should be no cracks in the dish; any water in them will turn to steam in the microwave and may break the dish apart.

Baked meat dishes

400 g/14 oz cabbage

500 g/18 oz potatoes, cooked
until still firm

2 shallots

salt

freshly ground pepper
from the mill

1 pinch sugar

1 tablespoon caraway seeds

1 tablespoon dried marjoram

2 tablespoons oil

4 spicy sausages

200 g/7 oz crème fraîche

200 ml/7 fl oz (⅞ cup) milk

4 eggs

75 g/3 oz (¾ cup) grated Gouda

Sausage gratin
with cabbage

This nourishing sausage gratin is very quick and easy to prepare, most of the work being done by the oven. To add special touch, sprinkle some crushed pretzels on top. It is delicious accompanied by a cold beer.

❶ Chop the cabbage coarsely with a large knife. Peel the potatoes and cut into cubes of about 1 cm/⅜ in. Peel the shallots and chop finely. Mix together the potatoes, shallots and cabbage. Add the sugar, caraway seeds and marjoram and season with salt, pepper.

❷ Heat the oil in a pan and fry the sausages until brown. Remove from the pan and cut into finger-thick slices. Stir into the cabbage mixture.

❸ Whisk together the crème fraîche, milk and eggs and season generously with salt and pepper.

❹ Transfer the cabbage mixture into a shallow gratin dish and pour the cream mixture on top. Sprinkle the grated cheese on top.

❺ Pre-heat the oven to 180°C (350°F), Gas mark 4 and bake for about 50 minutes until the potatoes are done.

Serves 4. About 695 kcal per serving.

Moussaka

Here tagliatelle is used to make the moussaka, but other kinds of pasta can be used instead, including wholewheat pasta. It is important that the pasta should retain a definite bite at the end of the pre-cooking stage because it would otherwise become too soft when baked.

1 Wash the aubergines (eggplants), remove the stalks and cut into slices about 2 cm/¾ in thick. Arrange on kitchen paper and sprinkle with salt. Peel the onions and chop finely. Peel the garlic and crush it.

2 For the sauce, heat 4 tablespoons oil in a sauté pan, add the onions and garlic and fry over medium heat until they become transparent. Increase the temperature, add the minced meat and continue frying while stirring. Cut the tomatoes into small pieces and add to the pan together with the juice. Wash the herbs, pat dry, remove the leaves from the stalks and add to the pan. Season generously with salt, pepper and sugar and simmer gently for about for 20 minutes.

3 Meanwhile, cook the tagliatelle in plenty of salted water until "al dente". Drain, plunge in cold water and drain again.

4 Heat 4 tablespoons oil in a pan. Dry the slices of aubergines with kitchen paper and fry on both sides, a few slices at a time.

5 Grease a gratin dish with the rest of the oil and add half the tagliatelle. Arrange alternate layers of sauce and aubergines on top and cover with the remaining tagliatelle.

6 Beat the eggs and cream together and season generously with salt, pepper and nutmeg. Pour over the tagliatelle and sprinkle Parmesan on top.

7 Preheat the oven to 200°C (400°F), Gas mark 6 and bake for about 40 minutes until golden brown.

Serves 6. About 940 kcal per serving.

4 small aubergines (eggplants)

salt

1 clove garlic

2 onions

10 tablespoons olive oil

500 g/18 oz minced meat

2 cans tomatoes, 400 g/14 oz each

1 sprig rosemary

2 sprigs thyme

freshly ground pepper from the mill

500 g/18 oz tagliatelle

4 eggs

250 ml/8 fl oz (1 cup) cream

freshly ground nutmeg

100 g/3½ oz (⅞ cup) freshly grated Parmesan

Shepherd's pie

8 medium potatoes

3 tablespoons butter

100 ml/3½ fl oz (½ cup) milk

1 onion

3 cloves garlic

2 tablespoons olive oil

1 kg/2¼ lb minced meat

3 tablespoons Worcestershire
   sauce

2 tablespoons flour

freshly ground pepper
   from the mill

❶ Peel the potatoes and boil for 20–30 minutes until soft. Drain. Using a fork or potato masher, mash in a bowl with the butter and milk, or use the blender.

❷ Peel and finely chop the onion and garlic. Heat the oil in a pan and sweat the garlic and onion until translucent. Add the minced meat, Worcestershire sauce and flour. Season with pepper and mix all together. Cover and leave to cook for about 15 minutes.

❸ Fill a casserole dish evenly with the mixture. Cover with the mashed potato. Cook on the middle shelf of the oven preheated to 200°C (400°F), Gas mark 6 for 45–50 minutes until the top is golden brown.

Serves 8. About 465 kcal per serving.

Kohlrabi gratin with turkey breast

The addition of herb curd cheese makes this gratin particularly creamy. Served with potato purée, it is also very popular with children.

750 g/1½ lb kohlrabi

salt

500 g/18 oz turkey breast
   escalopes

2 tablespoons oil

freshly ground pepper
   from the mill

1 large onion

250 ml/8 fl oz (1 cup) cream

150 g/5 oz (⅝ cup) curd cheese
   with herbs

freshly ground nutmeg

❶ Peel the kohlrabi, cut into thin slices and blanch in boiling salted water for about 2 to 3 minutes. Plunge in cold water and drain.

❷ Cut the escalopes into thin strips. Heat the oil in a pan and fry the meat briskly on all sides over high heat. Season with salt and pepper.

❸ Peel the onions, chop finely and fry in the remaining cooking juices. Stir in the cream and curd cheese and bring gently to the boil and simmer briefly to thicken the sauce. Season with salt, pepper and nutmeg.

❹ Arrange alternate layers of kohlrabi and meat in a greased gratin dish. Pour the cheese mixture on top.

❺ Preheat the oven to 200°C (400°F), Gas mark 6 and bake on the middle shelf for about 45 minutes.

Serves 4. About 445 kcal per serving.

Little gratiné veal roulades

These delicious little roulades immediately conjure up pictures of wonderful holidays in Italy. They can be prepares the day before and kept in the refrigerator. It is a perfect summer dish, delicious served with salad and ciabatta.

❶ Wash the celery stalks. Trim them and cut into pieces10 cm/4 in long and 1 cm/⅜ in across. Blanch for about 2 minutes in boiling salted water, plunge into very cold water and drain. Wash and trim the spring onions and peppers and cut into strips.

❷ Drain the tuna fish in a sieve and puree in a blender together with the crème fraîche, olive oil, anchovy fillets and capers. Wash the parsley and chives and pat dry. Chop the parsley leaves finely, and cut the chives into small rings. Stir the herbs into the tuna fish paste and season with salt and pepper.

❸ Put the veal pieces flat on a work top and season lightly with salt and pepper. Coat with the tuna fish paste, leaving the edge free. Place the vegetable strips on top. Roll them up l and secure with cocktail sticks.

❹ Heat the oil in non-stick pan until very hot and fry the roulades briefly.

❺ Grease a shallow gratiné dish with 1 tablespoon butter, arrange the veal roulades in it and sprinkle with Parmesan. Melt the rest of the butter and pour on top. Pre-heat the oven to 180°C (350°F), Gas mark 4 and bake on the second shelf from the top for about 15 minutes.

Serves 4. About 510 kcal per serving.

4 sticks celery

salt

8 spring onions

1 sweet red pepper

1 sweet yellow pepper

1 150 g/5 oz can tuna fish without oil

1 tablespoon crème fraîche

1 tablespoon olive oil

3 pickled anchovy fillets

1 tablespoon capers

½ bunch flat-leaved parsley

½ bunch chives

freshly ground white pepper from the mill

12 thin veal escalopes

2 tablespoons oil

4 tablespoons butter

75 g/3 oz (¾ cup) freshly grated Parmesan

Gratiné curried bananas with bacon

400 g/14 oz potatoes

300 g/10 oz frozen broccoli

4 tomatoes

150 g/5 oz bacon

4 large bananas

1 tablespoon mild curry powder

200 ml/7 fl oz (⅞ cup) cream

salt

freshly ground pepper
   from the mill

1 tablespoon oil

100 g/3½ oz (scant cup)
   grated Gouda

In Asia bananas are mainly used in savoury dishes. The addition of curry powder adds an exotic touch to this delicious gratin that will delight family and friends. Other vegetables such as sliced carrots may be used instead of broccoli.

❶ Wash the potatoes, boil and leave to cool. Peel and cut into thin slices. Defrost the broccoli and separate into small florets. Cut a cross in the tomatoes, blanch in boiling water and peel. Cut the tomatoes into quarters, remove the stalk and seeds and cut into large cubes.

❷ Cut the bacon into strips and fry until crisp in a non-stick frying-pan without any oil. Drain on kitchen paper.

❸ Cut each banana once lengthways, halve diagonally and fry in the remaining bacon fat. Remove from the pan. Sprinkle the curry powder in the pan, fry briefly and stir in the cream. Season with salt an pepper.

❹ Grease a shallow gratin dish with oil. Arrange the slices potatoes, broccoli, tomato cubes, pieces of bananas, half the cheese and the bacon. Pour the curried cream sauce on top.

❺ Preheat the oven to 200°C (400°F), Gas mark 6 and bake for about 25 minutes. Ten minutes before the end of the cooking time, sprinkle the rest of the bacon and cheese on top.

Serves 4. About 550 kcal per serving.

500 g/18 oz carrots

salt

500 g mushrooms

4 tablespoons oil

2 pork fillets, about 600 g/1¼ lb
in total

1 clove garlic

2 shallots

30 g/1 oz (2 tablespoons) butter

30 g/1 oz (¼ cup) flour

250 ml/8 fl oz (1 cup) veal or
vegetable stock (broth)

100 ml/3½ fl oz (½ cup) milk

125 g/4½ oz (⅝ cup) cream cheese

2 tablespoons coarsely crushed
pepper

2 tablespoons brandy

2 tablespoons dried parsley

Pork fillet with a pepper crust and vegetables

This gratin is perfect for guests and it looks particularly attractive when served in little ramekins. Crush the pepper corns in a mortar just before serving so that the full aroma is enjoyed. It is delicious served with creamed potato purée or a crusty baguette.

❶ Wash the carrots, peel, cut diagonally into thin slices and blanch for 7 minutes in boiling salted water. Plunge into very cold water and drain. Wipe the mushrooms clean with kitchen paper, trim and cut into slices. Heat 2 tablespoons oil in a non-stick pan, add the mushrooms and fry until golden-brown. Remove from the pan.

❷ Trim the pork fillets, remove all the skin, wash and pat dry. Cut in half and fry briefly but briskly in the rest of the oil over a high heat. Reduce the heat and continue frying the thinner pieces for about 8 minutes and the rest of the meat for about 10 minutes. Remove from the pan and put to one side.

❸ Peel the shallots and chop finely. Peel and crush the garlic.

❹ Melt the butter in the same pan until it foams and fry the shallots and garlic until they become transparent. Stir in the flour and fry until golden. Add the stock and milk, stirring constantly, and simmer gently for about 5 minutes. Stir in half the curd cheese, the crushed pepper corns and brandy. Season with salt.

❺ Cut the fillets into finger-thick slices. Put the vegetables in a shallow gratin dish, arrange the meat on top and pour the sauce over it. Sprinkle the parsley and the rest of the curd cheese in small flakes on top.

❻ Preheat the oven to 200°C (400°F), Gas mark 6 and bake for about 15 minutes.

Serves 4. About 520 kcal per serving.

White cabbage and minced meat gratin

This is a delicious gratin whose taste varies depending on whether minced beef, lamb or mutton is used.

❶ Remove the outer leaves of the white cabbage, remove the stalk and cut the rest into four. Wash the cabbage and cut into strips about 1 cm/⅜ in wide .

❷ Peel the onions and chop finely. Heat the oil in a pan, add the chopped onions and fry until transparent. Add the minced meat and fry for about 5 minutes. Then add the cabbage, salt, pepper and paprika and fry for another 30 minutes.

❸ Put the cabbage and minced meat in a greased gratin dish. Stir the stock into the tomato purée and pour it over the cabbage and meat mixture. Sprinkle cheese on top.

❹ Whisk the eggs, add the milk and a pinch of salt. Stir well and pour this milk and egg mixture over the gratin.

❺ Preheat the oven to 180°C (350°F), Gas mark 4 and bake on the middle shelf for about 20–30 minutes.

Serves 4 to 6. About 590 kcal per serving.

1 white cabbage

2 onions

6 tablespoons olive oil

300 g/10 oz minced meat

salt

freshly ground pepper
  from the mill

2 teaspoons paprika

250 ml/8 fl oz (1 cup) meat
  stock (broth)

3 tablespoons tomato puree

100 g/3½ oz (1 cup) freshly
  grated Gouda

3 eggs

250 ml/8 fl oz (1 cup) milk

Swiss bread gratin with turkey

This particular dish combines two delicious Swiss specialities. The golden-brown Swiss cheese conceals a *Geschnetzelte*, a mouth-watering dish consisting of small, thin slices of meat. It is delicious served with a baguette that can be dipped in the sauce.

1 Peel the onion and chop finely. Peel the garlic and press it in a garlic press. Wipe the mushrooms with kitchen paper, trim and cut into thin slices.

2 Heat the oil in a non-stick pan and fry the meat until brown. Remove from the pan. Reduce the temperature, add the chopped onion and garlic and fry until transparent. Add the mushrooms and fry briefly. Sprinkle with paprika and fry briefly. Stir in the cream and stock and simmer for another 5 minutes.

3 Add a little water to the thickening agent and stir until a smooth mixture is obtained. Stir this mixture into the sauce to thicken it. Add the meat and season with salt and pepper. Remove from the heat.

4 Cut the baguette into finger-thick slices and grate the cheese coarsely. Beat the eggs and milk together, season with salt and pepper.

5 Place the meat in an oval gratin dish and arrange the baguette slices on top so that they overlap. Sprinkle cheese on top and pour over the egg and milk mixture.

6 Preheat the oven to 200°C (400°F), Gas mark 6. and bake on the middle shelf for about 30 minutes until golden-brown.

Serves 4. About 570 kcal per serving.

1 large onion, 2 cloves garlic

200 g/7 oz mushrooms

2 tablespoons oil

400 g/14 oz turkey breast escalopes, cut into small pieces

1 tablespoon paprika

200 ml/7 fl oz (⅞ cup) cream

500 ml/17 fl oz (2¼ cups) veal or vegetable stock (broth)

1 tablespoon thickening agent, such as cornflour

salt, freshly ground pepper from the mill

½ baguette

120 g/4 oz medium hard cheese such as Appenzell or Gruyère

250 ml/8 fl oz (1 cup) milk

2 eggs

100 g/3½ oz bacon

1 very thick slice ham, about 100 g/3½ oz

500 g/18 oz ricotta

125 ml/4 fl oz (½ cup) milk

3 tablespoons thickening agent

3 eggs, separated

75 g/3 oz (3/4 cup) freshly grated Parmesan

salt

freshly ground pepper from the mill

freshly ground nutmeg

½ bunch parsley

½ bunch chives

1 tablespoon butter

2 tablespoons breadcrumbs

Ham and ricotta soufflé

In appearance this gratin looks much like a sweet soufflé, but in fact it is a nourishing dish prepared with bacon and ham. This can be replaced with chopped, fried vegetables to make a vegetarian dish.

❶ Cut the bacon into thin strips and fry in a non-stick pan without fat until crisp. Cut the ham into small cubes and fry with the bacon.

❷ For the soufflé mixture, stir the ricotta and milk together into a smooth mixture. Add the thickening agent (such as cornflour), egg yolks and Parmesan. Season generously with salt, pepper and nutmeg. Wash the parsley and chives and pat dry. Chop the parsley leaves finely, cut the chives into small rings and add to the soufflé mixture.

❸ Beat the egg whites with a pinch of salt until stiff and carefully fold into the soufflé mixture.

❹ Grease a gratin dish with butter. Gently pour the mixture into it and smooth out the surface. Sprinkle with breadcrumbs.

❺ Preheat the oven to 200°C (400°F), Gas mark 6 and bake on the middle shelf for about 25 to 30 minutes until golden-brown. Do not open the oven while cooking.

Serves 4. About 495 kcal per serving.

Chicken risotto gratin

This gratin is ideal for using up chicken left-overs. If there also happens to be some risotto left over, this otherwise quite elaborate dish can be prepared in no time at all.

1 Cut the chicken breasts into thin strips. Add 2 tablespoons of oil and a little pepper to the lemon juice and stir. Pour the marinade over the meat, stir well and leave in the refrigerator for about 2 hours.

2 Stir together the stock and wine, add the bay leaves and bring to the boil. Peel the onion and chop finely. Heat 1 tablespoon of oil in a pan and fry the chopped onion until transparent. Add the rice and curry powder and stir.

3 Add the wine and stock mixture little by little to the rice, using a ladle, stirring continuously until the liquid has been absorbed. Add another ladle of the liquid and stock and continue stirring until all the liquid has evaporated. Repeat the operation until the rice is cooked, probably about 20 minutes.

4 Wash and trim the courgettes. Grate three-quarters of the amount coarsely and cut the remainder into slices. Cut the mozzarella cheese into slices. Stir the cream and grated courgettes into the cooked rice. Season with salt and pepper.

5 Put the rice mixture in a greased gratin dish. Arrange the meat on top and garnish with the sliced courgettes and mozzarella. Season again with salt and pepper and dot with flakes of butter.

6 Preheat the oven to 220°C (425°F), Gas mark 7 and bake on the middle shelf for about 20 minutes.

Serves 4. About 580 kcal per serving.

200 g/7 oz chicken breasts

1 tablespoon lemon juice

3 tablespoons sunflower oil

freshly ground pepper
  from the mill

500 ml/17 fl oz (2¼ cups) chicken
  stock (broth)

450 ml/15 fl oz (2 cups) dry white
  wine

2 bay leaves

1 small onion

200 g/7 oz (1 cup) risotto rice

1 tablespoon curry powder

3 courgettes (zucchini)

200 g/7 oz mozzarella

125 ml/4 fl oz (½ cup) cream

salt

1 tablespoon butter

Mexican sausage gratin

This interesting gratin is very spicy, hiding a fiery filling under its mild quark topping. Instead of sausages, left-over roast meat may be used. Vegetarians can replace the meat with a small tin of red kidney beans.

750 g/1½ lb potatoes

4 sausages

1 sweet red pepper

1 sweet yellow pepper

1 small can sweetcorn

1 onion

2 cloves garlic

100 g/3½ oz bacon

4 tablespoons olive oil

salt

freshly ground pepper from the mill,

1 pinch chilli powder

1 small can tomatoes

3 eggs, separated

250 g/9 oz quark (20% fat)

50 g/2 oz (½ cup) semolina flour

1 bunch chives

100 g/3½ oz (⅞ cup) grated hard cheese

❶ Boil the potatoes so that they are still firm, not floury. Drain and leave them to cool.

❷ Cut the sausages into thin slices. Wash the peppers, trim, remove the stalks and cut into small cubes. Drain the corn. Peel the onion, cut in half and slice into thin strips. Peel the garlic and crush in a garlic press. Cut the bacon into thin strips.

❸ Heat 3 tablespoons oil in a non-stick pan, add the onions and garlic and fry over a low flame until transparent. Increase the temperature, add the vegetables, sliced sausages and bacon and continue frying. Add the chopped tomatoes (reserving the juice) and cook for a little while until the mixture thickens. Season generously with salt, pepper and chilli powder.

❹ For the quark mixture, stir together the egg yolks, quark and semolina flour. Season generously with salt and pepper. Wash the chives, pat dry, cut into thin rings and add to the mixture. Beat the egg whites stiff and fold carefully into the quark mixture.

❺ Peel the potatoes and cut into slices 5 mm/³⁄₁₆ in thick. Grease a gratin dish with the rest of the oil.

❻ Arrange half the sliced potatoes on the bottom of the dish and cover with half the vegetable and sausage mixture. Add the remaining potatoes and arrange so that they overlap. Sprinkle with cheese.

❼ Preheat the oven to 200°C (400°F), Gas mark 6 and bake on the middle shelf for about 40 minutes until golden-brown.

Serves 6. About 580 kcal per serving.

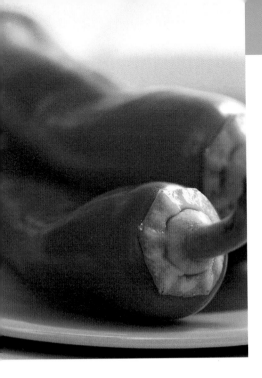

Veal and vegetable gratin

If this gratin is for more than 4 people, more vegetables can be added to increase the quantity: for instance, 150 g/5 oz carrots, 3 potatoes and 250 g/9 oz green beans. The dish is delicious served with rice or simply with crusty white bread.

500 g/18 oz veal from the leg

3 onions

2 cloves garlic

3 tomatoes

3 tablespoons olive oil

salt

**freshly ground pepper
    from the mill**

2 teaspoons paprika

2 aubergines (eggplants)

2 courgettes (zucchini)

3 sweet yellow peppers

2 chillies

1 tablespoon butter

❶ Cut the meat into cubes of about 3 cm/1¼ in. Peel the onions and garlic. Chop the onions coarsely and the garlic finely. Wash the tomatoes and make a cross-shaped cut. Blanch briefly in boiling water and peel. Cut the tomatoes into quarters, remove the stalk and chop into small pieces.

❷ Heat the oil in a pan, add the onions and garlic and fry. Now add the meat and fry until brown. Then add the tomatoes and braise for another 5 minutes. Season with salt, pepper and paprika.

❸ Wash the aubergines and courgettes and cut into cubes of about 2 cm/¾ in. Wash the peppers, trim, cut in half, remove the seeds and cut them too into cubes of 2 cm/¾ in. Wash the chillies, trim and cut into slices.

❹ Stir all the vegetables together and place in a greased gratin dish. Arrange the meat and tomato mixture on top. Pour ½ cup of water over the gratin and add the butter in flakes.

❺ Preheat the oven to 180°C (350°F), Gas mark 4 and bake on the middle shelf for 40–50 minutes.

Serves 4–6. About 280 kcal per serving.

Baked onion and meat gratin

This is an ideal way to stretch the left-overs from the Sunday roast. It is delicious served with crisp white bread and a green salad, washed down with a glass of red wine. If people are particularly hungry, it may be served with a creamy potato purée.

❶ Cut the meat into thin slices. Peel the onions and cut into half. Cut one half into rings and the other half into small cubes.

❷ Melt half the butter in a pan until it begins to foam. Add the onion rings and fry until golden-brown, then remove from the pan. Next melt the rest of the butter, add the chopped onions, cover and sweat over a low heat so that they become transparent without turning golden or brown. Add a little wine now and again.

❸ Add the crème fraîche and the rest of the wine. Reduce the liquid. Purée with a hand-mixer and season with salt, sugar, pepper and balsamic vinegar.

❹ Arrange the slices of roast meat and onion rings in alternate layers in a shallow gratin dish, pour the onion sauce on top and sprinkle with Parmesan. Preheat the oven to 220°C (425°F), Gas mark 7 and bake on the middle shelf for about 15 minutes.

Serves 4. About 465 kcal per serving.

400–500 g/14–18 oz left-over roast meat

6 onions

50 g/2 oz (4 tablespoons) butter

100 ml/3½ fl oz (½ cup) dry white wine

100 ml/3½ fl oz (½ cup) crème fraîche

salt

1 pinch sugar

freshly ground white pepper

1 tablespoon dried marjoram

2 tablespoons balsamic vinegar

75 g/3 oz (¾ cup) freshly grated Parmesan

Spicy lamb cutlets

Depending on taste, this dish can be made with a mild cheese like Gouda or a stronger one like Gruyère. For a less spicy dish, the amount of paprika may be reduced.

1 Peel the onions and cut into rings. Wash the tomatoes, make a cross-shaped cut, blanch briefly in boiling water and peel. Cut the tomatoes into quarters, remove the stalks and cut into cubes. Wash the chillies, cut in half and remove the seeds.

2 Melt 1 tablespoon butter in a pan and fry the onion rings. Add the tomatoes and cook for about 5 minutes. Add the chillies and simmer for another 1–2 minutes.

3 Put the cutlets in a greased gratin dish and pour over the vegetable mixture. Season with salt, thyme and paprika and sprinkle cheese on top.

4 Preheat the oven to 180°C (350°F), Gas mark 4 and bake on the middle shelf for 30–40 minutes.

Serves 4. About 280 kcal per serving.

2 onions

4 tomatoes

4 chillies

2 tablespoons butter

12 lamb cutlets

salt

1 tablespoon dried thyme

1 tablespoon paprika

75 g/3 oz (¾ cup) freshly grated cheese (Gouda or Gruyère)

Baked minced lamb balls

These meat balls are particularly full of flavour because of the minced lamb, but other meat may be used if preferred. This dish is excellent served with tagliatelle or pitta bread and salad.

1 onion

1 clove garlic

500 g/18 oz minced lamb

1 egg

1 tablespoon dried thyme

salt

freshly ground pepper
    from the mill

1 tablespoon paprika

200 ml/7 fl oz (⅞ cup) crème
    fraîche

1 small can tomatoes

1 bunch basil

2 balls mozzarella

❶ Peel the onion and garlic. Chop the onions finely and crush the garlic in a garlic press.

❷ Add the garlic, onion and egg to the minced lamb and knead well to incorporate all the ingredients. Season generously with thyme, salt, pepper and paprika. Moisten the hands and roll the mixture into small meat balls. Arrange them in a shallow gratin dish.

❸ Stir together the crème fraîche, coarsely chopped tomatoes and tomato juice. Season with salt and pepper. Wash the basil and pat dry. Reserve a dozen leaves for the garnish and chop the rest finely. Stir into the tomato and cream mixture. Pour this sauce over the meat balls.

❹ Cut the mozzarella into slices and pale them over the meat balls. Preheat the oven to 200°C (400°F), Gas mark 6. and bake on the middle shelf for about 25 minutes. Garnish with the rest of the basil leaves before serving.

Serves 4. About 660 kcal per serving.

Greek minced meat gratin

Lamb and feta (ewes' milk cheese) are both very popular in Greece. This dish may also be made from a mixture of minced beef and pork, which is excellent but less authentic. Either way, it is delicious on a summer's day, served with pitta bread and salad. On a very hot day, it can be served cold, accompanied by a bowl of black olives and chilli paste.

❶ Wash the courgettes (zucchini) and spring onions, trim and cut into pieces 3–4 cm/1¼–1½ in long. Peel the potatoes and cut into four or eight pieces depending on their size.

❷ Heat 2 tablespoons oil in a non-stick pan, add the courgettes and spring onions, fry until golden brown and remove from the pan. Add the potatoes to the pan and fry for about 10 minutes, turning regularly. Remove from the pan.

❸ Heat 2 more tablespoons oil in the pan, add the minced meat and fry for about 5 minutes. Add the tomato purée. Wash the thyme, pat dry, remove the leaves from the stalks and chop finely. Add the chopped thyme to the minced meat and season generously with salt, pepper and paprika. Remove from the heat and add the fried vegetables. Wash the tomatoes, remove the stalks, cut each into eight pieces and add to the minced meat mixture.

❹ Put this mixture in a gratin dish. Crumble the feta and sprinkle over the gratin.

❺ Whisk together the sour cream and eggs and season with salt and pepper. Pour over the gratin and sprinkle the rest of the olive oil over the top.

❻ Preheat the oven to 200°C (400°F), Gas mark 6 and bake on the middle shelf for about 20 minutes until golden brown. Wash the parsley, pat dry and chop the leaves coarsely. Sprinkle on the gratin just before serving.

Serves 4. About 955 kcal per serving.

4 small courgettes (zucchini)

1 bunch spring onions

750 g/1½ lb potatoes

8 tablespoons olive oil

500 g/18 oz minced lamb

2 tablespoons tomato puree

2 sprigs thyme

salt

freshly ground pepper
   from the mill

1 pinch paprika

3 beef tomatoes

200 g/7 oz feta (Greek ewes'
   milk cheese)

200 ml/7 fl oz (⅞ cup) sour cream

2 eggs

1 bunch flat-leaved parsley

Chicken breast with creamed onions

The delicate creamed onion sauce makes this gratin a very special dish. Instead of potatoes, polenta slices may be used and mild mozzarella can replace the Parmesan.

750 g/1½ lb potatoes

1 400 g/14 oz can tomatoes

4 chicken breasts, without skin

2 tablespoons oil

2 onions

1 clove garlic

125 ml/4 fl oz (½ cup) chopped chicken

200 ml/7 fl oz (⅞ cup) cream

2 tablespoons thickening agent (such as cornflour)

salt

freshly ground pepper from the mill

1 pinch sugar

2 tablespoons medium sherry

2 sprigs thyme

1 tablespoon butter

100 g/3½ oz (⅞ cup) freshly grated Parmesan

❶ Wash the potatoes and boil in their skins until firm but not floury. Leave to cool. Drain the tomatoes and cut into small pieces. Reserve the juice.

❷ Wash the chicken fillets, pat dry and fry briskly in hot oil for about 2 minutes on each side. Remove from the pan. Peel the onions, cut in half and cut into thin slices. Peel the garlic and crush.

❸ Reduce the heat, add the slices of onion and crushed garlic and fry until soft and golden. Add the chicken stock and cream. Add the thickening agent to thicken the sauce. Add the tomatoes and season with salt, pepper, sugar and sherry. Wash the thyme, pat dry, remove the leaves and stir into the sauce.

❹ Peel the potatoes and cut into thin slices. Grease a shallow gratin dish with butter and arrange the slices of potatoes around the edge so that they overlap and place the chicken fillets in the middle. Pour the sauce over top and sprinkle the Parmesan over all.

❺ Preheat the oven to 200°C (400°F), Gas mark 6 and bake on the middle shelf for about 20 minutes.

Serves 4. About 640 kcal per serving.

Gratin of smoked pork loin and sprouts

This is a delicious variation on a popular dish, ideal for a cold winter's day. It is made with smoked loin of pork, a German speciality known as Kassler. To save time, a ready-made cheese sauce and frozen vegetables may be used. The dish is also delicious made with leeks instead of Brussels sprouts.

❶ Boil the potatoes so that they are still firm, not floury, drain and leave to cool. Wash and trim the sprouts and cook "al dente". Drain, plunge in very cold water and drain again.

❷ Cut the smoked pork loin into 1.5 cm/½ in pieces. Peel the onions and chop them finely.

❸ Melt the butter in a pan until it begins to foam. Fry the onions until they become transparent. Sprinkle the flour on top and fry until golden. Add the stock and cream and simmer gently for about 5 more minutes. Stir in the caraway seeds and half the cheese. Season with salt and pepper

❹ Peel the potatoes, cut into half and put in a shallow gratin dish together with the sprouts and pork loin and pour the cheese sauce over it. Sprinkle the rest of the cheese on top.

❺ Preheat the oven to 200°C (400°F), Gas mark 6 and bake on the middle shelf for about 20 minutes until golden brown.

Serves 4. About 830 kcal per serving.

1 kg/2¼ lb small potatoes, cooked until still firm

800 g/1¾ lb Brussels sprouts

salt

4 slices cooked smoked pork loin

50 g/2 oz (4 tablespoons) butter butter

1 onion

50 g/2 oz (½ cup) flour

200 ml/7 fl oz (⅞ cup) vegetable stock (broth)

200 ml/7 fl oz (⅞ cup) cream

1 tablespoon caraway seeds

100 g/31/2 oz (⅞ cup) grated Gouda

freshly ground pepper from the mill

Baked
fish dishes

800 g/1¾ lb fish fillet, such as pollack or cod

juice of 1 lemon

salt

350 g/12 oz tomatoes

20 g/¾ oz (1½ tablespoons) butter

3 eggs

125 ml/4 fl oz (½ cup) cream

2 teaspoons green peppercorns

1 tablespoon chopped parsley

Fish gratin with peppercorns

This dish with green peppercorns will delight everyone who love spicy food. It is delicious with boiled potatoes and a green salad.

❶ Wash the fish fillets thoroughly, wipe dry and sprinkle with lemon juice and salt.

❷ Wash the tomatoes, make a cross-shaped cut at the top, blanch in boiling water and peel. Cut the tomatoes into quarters, remove the stalks and cut into slices.

❸ Grease a gratin dish with butter and arrange alternate layers of tomato slices and fish fillets.

❹ Stir the eggs, peppercorns and parsley into the cream and pour over the gratin. Cover with aluminium foil.

❺ Preheat the oven to 220°C (425°F), Gas mark 7 and bake on the middle shelf for about 30 minutes.

Serves 4. About 350 kcal per serving.

Mussels gratin

This dish is ideal for impatient mussel-lovers because the mussels have already been removed from their shells in the kitchen. You can also add other ingredients to the mussels such as previously-cooked diced potatoes. The dish is delicious served with fresh bread, accompanied by a glass of dry white wine.

❶ Wash the mussels several times, scrub thoroughly clean and remove all the filaments and parasites. Fill a large pan with a little water, add a pinch of salt and bring to the boil. Add the mussels, cover and cook for about 8 – 10 minutes until the shells have all opened. Pour the cooking liquid through a sieve and reserve. Remove the mussels from their shells and throw away any that have not opened.

❷ Wash the peppers, remove stalk and seeds and cut into small cubes. Peel the cloves of garlic and push through a garlic press. Heat the oil in a pan, add the peppers and garlic and fry. Cut the ham into cubes and add to the pan. Add some flour, stir well and allow to brown. Next add the cooking liquid and wine and simmer for about 5 minutes.

❸ Add the peas, mussels and crème fraîche and season generously with salt and pepper.

❹ Pour the mussels mixture into a gratin dish and sprinkle with Parmesan. Preheat the oven to 220°C (425°F), Gas mark 7 and bake on the second shelf from the top for about 10 minutes until golden-brown.

Serves 4. About 475 kcal per serving.

1.5 kg/3¼ lb mussels, salt

1 sweet red pepper, 1 sweet green pepper

2 cloves garlic

2 tablespoons olive oil

2 slices cooked ham (100 g/3½ oz each)

30 g/1 oz (¼ cup) flour

100 ml/3½ fl oz (½ cup) dry white wine

300 g/10 oz frozen peas

100 ml/3½ fl oz (½ cup) crème fraîche

freshly ground pepper from the mill

75 g/3 oz (¾ cup) freshly grated Parmesan

Gratiné zander on a bed of ratatouille

This gratin looks particularly sophisticated with its decorative potato purée topping and is therefore ideal for special occasions. Other kinds of white fish fillets may be used instead of zander, and leeks are a possible alternative for the ratatouille.

1 sweet red pepper

1 sweet yellow pepper

2 small courgettes (zucchini)

1 small aubergine (eggplant)

1 onion

2 cloves garlic

1 can peeled tomatoes

3 tablespoons olive oil

2 sprigs thyme

1 sprig rosemary

salt

freshly ground pepper
  from the mill

1 packet instant potato (3
  helpings)

125 ml/4 fl oz (½ cup) milk

600 g/1¼ lb zander fillet

30 g/1 oz (2 tablespoons) butter

❶ Trim the peppers, wash and cut into thin strips. Trim the courgettes, wash and cut into slices 1 cm/⅜ in thick . Wash the aubergines, remove the stalk and cut into cubes of 1 cm/⅜ in. Peel the onion, cut in half, then into thin strips. Peel the cloves of garlic and push through a garlic press.

❷ Heat the olive oil in a pan, add the onion and garlic and fry over a low heat until transparent. Add the prepared vegetables, increase the heat and fry. Drain the tomatoes, cut into small pieces (reserving the juice) and add to the pan. Wash the thyme and rosemary and pat dry. Pull the leaves off the stems, chop them finely and add to the pan. Season with salt and pepper. Simmer gently until the vegetables are "al dente".

❸ Make the potato purée with milk following the instructions on the packet and pour into an icing bag with a large nozzle. Arrange the zander fillets in shallow gratin dish, greased with butter. Place the vegetables on top and pipe the potato purée in wavy lines to cover the vegetables. Dot with flakes of butter.

❹ Preheat the oven to 220°C (425°F), Gas mark 7 and bake on the middle shelf for about for about 20 minutes.

Serves 4. About 330 kcal per serving.

Baked sardines

Sardines are ideal for baking because their high fat content prevents them from drying out. This dish is popular in Mediterranean countries and it is very quick and easy to prepare. It is an ideal starter for a summer menu.

750 g/1½ lb fresh sardines, cooked

juice of 1 lemon

4 tablespoons olive oil

1 untreated lemon

salt

freshly ground pepper from the mill

200 ml/7 fl oz (⅞ cup) dry white wine

2 sprigs thyme

1 bunch parsley

8 tablespoons fresh breadcrumbs

❶ Carefully scale the sardines and cut off the heads. Sprinkle with lemon juice.

❷ Choose a shallow gratin dish in which all the sardines will fit without overlapping and grease with 1 tablespoon of oil. Wash the lemon carefully, cut into slices and arrange at the bottom of the dish. Place the sardines on top.

❸ Season with salt and pepper and add the wine. Wash the thyme and parsley and pat dry. Remove the leaves from the stems, chop finely, mix together with the breadcrumbs and sprinkle over the fish. Pour the rest of the olive oil on top.

❹ Preheat the oven to the 180°C (350°F), Gas mark 4 and bake on the middle shelf for about 20 minutes. The sardines are ready when the fins on the back come off easily.

Serves 4. About 415 kcal per serving.

Herring gratin

People who enjoy herrings will be adore this dish. Instead of being served with a cold creamy sauce, here the herring fillets are baked in the oven. Herring gratin is delicious served with pickled beetroot.

❶ Boil the potatoes in their skins so that they are firm, not floury. Drain and leave to cool. Soak the herring fillets for at least 1 hour, pat dry and cut diagonally into strips about 3 cm/1¼ in wide . Peel the apple, cut into quarters, remove the core and cut into thin slices.

❷ Peel the potatoes and cut into thin slices. Arrange the sliced potatoes in a shallow gratin dish so that they overlap. Follow with the fish fillets, sliced apple and the remaining potatoes in layers.

❸ Stir together the eggs, sour cream and cream and season generously with salt, pepper and caraway seeds.

❹ Pour the egg and cream mixture over the gratin. Preheat the oven to 220°C (425°F), Gas mark 7 and bake on the middle shelf for about 30 minutes.

❺ Peel the onions and cut in very thin rings. Serve with the gratin together with the pickled gherkins.

Serves 4. About 710 kcal per serving.

1 kg/2¼ lb potatoes

4 raw herring fillets

1 sharp apple

2 eggs

200 ml/7 fl oz (⅞ cup) sour cream

200 ml/7 fl oz (⅞ cup) cream

salt

freshly ground pepper
    from the mill

1 tablespoon caraway seeds

2 red onion

4 pickled gherkins

Stuffed aubergines (eggplants)

This is a popular American recipe with crabmeat and shrimps. It is delicious served with salad and a crusty baguette.

2 large aubergines (eggplants)

1 can crabmeat

500 g/18 oz shrimps(cooked and peeled)

1 onion

1 sweet red pepper

2 tomatoes

2 cloves garlic

butter

3 oz/75g (1 cup) cooked rice

3 tablespoons chopped parsley

salt

pepper

50 g/2 oz (1/2 cup) grated Cheddar cheese

❶ Cut the aubergines (eggplants) in half, hollow out the flesh and chop into small pieces. Cut the shrimps and crabmeat into small pieces. Peel and dice the onion. Wash the sweet pepper and cut into dice. Put the tomatoes in boiling water, skin and dice too. Peel the garlic and chop finely.

❷ Melt the butter in a pan and cook the sweet pepper and onion for about 5 minutes. Add the flesh of the aubergine, tomatoes, garlic and rice and stir together. Leave to cook for 5 minutes, then add the shrimps. Season with parsley, salt and pepper.

❸ Fill the aubergine halves with the cooked mixture and sprinkle with grated Cheddar cheese.

❹ Put the stuffed aubergines in a buttered dish, sprinkle with water and cook in the oven preheated to 190°C (375°F), Gas mark 5 for about 30 minutes.

Serves 4. About 590 kcal per serving.

Fish gratin

Instead of the pollack as used in this recipe, other sea fish such as cod or haddock may be used. Freshwater fish such as trout is also excellent.

1 Wash the fish fillets thoroughly, wipe dry, sprinkle with lemon juice and season with salt and pepper. Cut into cubes of about 2 cm/¾ in. Defrost the prawns (shrimps).

2 Peel the onion and chop finely. Wash the spinach, trim and remove the thicker stems. Heat the oil in a pan and fry the onion until transparent. Add the spinach and braise until it collapses. Season with salt and pepper.

3 Melt the butter in a pan, add the flour, stir and cook until it turns golden. Next add the milk gradually, stirring all the time. Bring very slowly to the boil, season with salt and pepper and stir in the cheese.

4 Put the uncooked rice in a greased gratin dish and stir in the saffron. Place the fish fillets on the rice, cover with the spinach and sprinkle the prawns on top. Finally, pour the béchamel over all.

5 Preheat the oven to 200°C (400°F), Gas mark 6 and bake on the middle shelf for about 30 minutes.

Serves 4. About 345 kcal per serving.

400 g/14 oz pollack fillets

juice of ½ lemon

salt

freshly ground pepper from the mill

50 g/2 oz (⅜ cup) shelled prawns (shrimps)

1 onion

1 kg/2¼ lb spinach

1 tablespoon sunflower oil

10 g/⅓ oz (1½ tablespoons) flour

10 g/⅓ oz (½ tablespoon) butter

250 ml/8 fl oz (1 cup) milk

75 g/3 oz (¾ cup) Gouda, freshly grated

80 g/3 oz (scant ½ cup) rice

1 pinch saffron

Rose fish and leaf spinach gratin with breadcrumbs

It does take a little more time to use fresh spinach but it is worth it because fresh vegetables have a stronger flavour. The topping consists only of breadcrumbs so as not to overpower the taste. Choose your favourite herbs.

1 Wash the spinach thoroughly several times and trim carefully. Peel the shallots and chop finely. Peel the garlic and crush. Heat the olive oil in a large saucepan and sweat the shallots and garlic until transparent. Add the wet spinach and continue braising until the spinach collapses.

butter and stir until it foams. Add the lemon zest, herbs and breadcrumbs and stir well.

juice on the rose fish fillets. Put the spinach in a shallow the fish with salt and pepper and arrange on the spinach. large enough for the fish fillets to fit in it.

the fish and spinach with the breadcrumb-mixture. Preheat the C (400°F), Gas mark 6 and bake on the middle shelf for about 20

ut 370 kcal per serving.

1.5 kg/3¼ lb fresh spinach

1 shallot

1 clove garlic

2 tablespoons olive oil

2 tablespoons soft butter

juice and zest of 1 untreated lemon

4 tablespoons fresh, chopped herbs

8 tablespoons fresh breadcrumbs

800 g/1¾ lb rose fish fillet

4 beef tomatoes

2 small courgettes (zucchini)

2 sticks celery

1 bunch spring onions

1 clove garlic

4 tablespoons olive oil

2 sprigs thyme

½ bunch basil

½ bunch parsley

2 tablespoons tomato puree

125 g/4½ oz mascarpone

salt

freshly ground pepper from the
    mill

800 g/1¾ lb fish fillets, such as
    cod, catfish or red snapper

200 g/7 oz mozzarella

Fish fillet with mascarpone

The fish is beautifully juicy under the vegetable and cheese topping and the various flavours combine perfectly. If mascarpone is not available, crème fraîche may be used instead. The vegetables too may be changed according to what is in season, such as leaf spinach. This dish is delicious served with baked potatoes or crusty.crispy white bread.

❶ Make a cross-shaped cut in the tomatoes, blanch in boiling water and peel. Cut the tomatoes into quarters, remove the stalk and the seeds. Cut the flesh into small cubes. Trim the courgettes, celery and spring onions and wash. Cut the courgettes into small cubes, the celery sticks and spring onions into slices.

❷ Heat 3 tablespoons oil in a pan, add the vegetables and garlic and fry briefly. Remove from the heat. Wash the thyme, basil and parsley and pat dry. Remove the leaves from the stems and chop finely. Mix together the herbs, tomato purée and mascarpone. Season with salt and pepper.

❸ Grease a gratin dish with the rest of the oil and arrange the fish fillets in it. Season with salt and pepper. Cut the mozzarella into small cubes, add to the vegetable mixture and pour the vegetables over the fish. Preheat the oven to 220°C (425°F), Gas mark 7 and bake on the middle shelf for about 15 minutes.

Serves 4. About 550 kcal per serving.

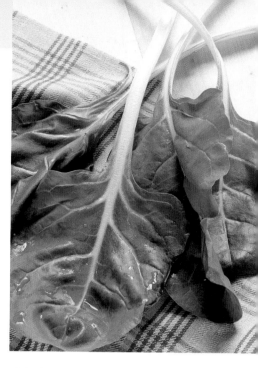

Cod and Swiss chard bake

Swiss chard, cod and cheese complement each other beautifully. But instead of Swiss chard, other vegetables such as leaf spinach or leeks may be used.

1 Wash the Swiss chard, drain, remove the stalks and cut the leaves into strips. Soften in boiling salted water and drain.

2 Make the potato with milk following the instructions on the package. Season with salt and pepper.

3 Cut the fish into individual portions and sprinkle with lemon juice.

4 Stir the eggs into the crème fraîche and season with salt and pepper. Then stir in 100 g/3½ oz (scant 1 cup) cheese into the mixture.

5 Grease a shallow gratin dish with butter and put the potato purée at the bottom with the Swiss chard on top. Arrange the fish fillets on the vegetables and pour the cheese sauce on top. Sprinkle with cheese.

6 Preheat the oven to 200°C (400°F), Gas mark 6 and bake on the middle shelf for about 20–25 minutes.

Serves 4. About 495 kcal per serving.

500 g/18 oz Swiss chard

salt

1 packet instant potato (3 helpings)

250 ml/8 fl oz (1 cup) milk

freshly ground pepper

freshly ground nutmeg

600 g/1¼ lb cod fillets

1 lemon

125 ml/4 fl oz (½ cup) crème fraîche

2 eggs

150 g/5 oz (1¼ cups) grated cheese

1 tablespoon butter

4 beef tomatoes

300 g/10 oz mushrooms

2 small leeks

2 shallots

2 cloves garlic

6 tablespoons olive oil

1 tablespoon tomato puree

salt

freshly ground pepper
    from the mill

1 pinch sugar

1 pinch chilli powder

1 bunch basil

½ bunch parsley

600 g/1¼ lb raw scampi (shrimps)
    in their shells

50 g/2 oz (½ cup) freshly grated
    Parmesan

2 tablespoons fresh breadcrumbs

Baked scampi

This scampi gratin, baked in a spicy tomato sauce, is clearly inspired by Mediterranean cuisine. It is an ideal evening meal for guests when time is short. It can be made even more special by adding a little cream to the sauce, which can be prepared the day before. Serve with rice or white crusty bread and salad.

❶ Make a cross-shaped cut in the tomatoes, blanch in boiling water and peel. Cut the tomatoes into quarters, remove the stalk and the seeds. Cut the flesh into cubes. Wipe the mushrooms clean with kitchen paper, trim and cut into quarters. Trim the leeks, wash thoroughly and cut the white and light green parts into rings about 1 cm/⅜ in thick. Peel the shallots and chop finely. Peel the garlic and crush in a garlic press.

❷ Heat 2 tablespoons oil in a non-stick pan, fry the mushrooms and leeks briefly and remove from the pan. Reduce the heat, add the chopped shallots and garlic and fry until transparent. Now add the diced tomatoes and tomato purée and simmer over a low flame for about 5 minutes. The sauce should be quite thick but if it is too thick a little water may be added. Season generously with salt, pepper, sugar and chilli powder.

❸ Wash the basil and parsley and pat dry. Pull the leaves from the stems, chop half of them finely and add to the tomato sauce.

❹ Shell the scampi, clean them and cut in half lengthways. Heat 2 tablespoons oil in a pan until very hot and then fry the scampi for 1 minute on each side. Remove from the pan.

❺ Put the scampi and vegetables in four small ramekins and pour the tomato sauce on top. Mix together the Parmesan and white breadcrumbs with the rest of the parsle, sprinkle on top and sprinkle the rest of the oil over it.

❻ Preheat the oven to 220°C (425°F), Gas mark 7 and bake on the second shelf from the top for about 10 minutes. Garnish with the rest of the basil just before serving.

Serves 4. About 390 kcal per serving.

Quick fish gratin with winter vegetables

This is the perfect dish for when time is short. It is undemanding because any kind of frozen vegetables and other kinds of fish such as pollack or rose fish may be used. It is delicious served with rice or potatoes.

800 g/1¾ lb cod fillets

juice of ½ lemon

2 tablespoons oil

450 g/1 lb frozen soup vegetables

salt

freshly ground pepper from the mill

20 g/3/4 oz (1½ tablespoons)

30 g/1 oz (¼ cup) flour

250 ml/8 fl oz (1 cup) milk

2 egg yolks

1 tablespoon horseradish

1 bunch dill

150 ml/5 fl oz (⅝ cup) cream

❶ Cut the fish fillets into four pieces of equal size and sprinkle with lemon juice.

❷ Heat the oil in a non-stick pan, add the defrosted vegetables, fry and season with salt and pepper.

❸ Melt the butter in a small pan until it begins to foam, add the flour and brown lightly. Add the milk slowly, stir carefully to avoid lumps and simmer for about 5 minutes. Season with salt and pepper and a dash of lemon juice. Remove from the heat and stir in the egg yolks and horseradish.

❹ Place the fish fillets in a shallow gratin dish and season with salt and pepper. Arrange the vegetables on top. Whisk the cream until stiff, add to the sauce and pour over the gratin.

❺ Preheat the oven to 200°C (400°F), Gas mark 6 and bake on the second shelf from the bottom for 25–30 minutes.

Serves 4. About 460 kcal per serving.

Baked fish fillet
on a bed of potatoes

Rose fish or pollack are ideal for this simple gratin. However, it is important that all the ingredients should be of top quality and in the case of the potatoes, choose waxy ones.

❶ Cut the fish fillets into individual portions and sprinkle with lemon juice. Peel the potatoes and cut into very thin slices, about as thick as a coin.

❷ Grease a shallow gratin dish with 1 tablespoon oil and arrange three-quarters of the potato slices overlapping in layers. Season generously with salt and pepper and pour 2 tablespoons olive oil over the potato slices. Preheat the oven to 200°C (400°F), Gas mark 6 and bake on the middle shelf for about 10 minutes.

❸ Wash the thyme and pat dry. Remove the leaves from the stems and chop coarsely. Take the gratin dish out of the oven, arrange the fish fillets on the potatoes and sprinkle with thyme. Now cover the fish with the rest of the potato slices, season again with salt and pepper, add the white wine and sprinkle the rest of the olive oil on top.

❹ Bake in the oven for a further 20–25 minutes at the same temperature. Wash the parsley, pat dry, chop the leaves finely and sprinkle over the gratin just before serving.

Serves 4. About 485 kcal per serving.

800 g/1¾ lb fish fillets

juice of 1 lemon

750 g/1½ lb potatoes, cooked until still firm, not floury

6 tablespoons olive oil

salt

freshly ground pepper from the mill

2 sprigs thyme

200 ml/7 fl oz (⅞ cup) dry white wine

½ bunch parsley

Baked vegetable dishes

Savoy cabbage gratin

This nourishing gratin is the perfect dish on a cold winter's day to revive everyone after a vigorous walk. You can also add Kassler ham, cut into small strips, to the gratin. If you are in a rush you can use instant potato purée/mashed potatoes.

1 kg/2¼ lb potatoes,

salt

1 small Savoy cabbage, about
   1 kg/2¼ lb

1 onion

100 g/3½ oz streaky bacon

3 tablespoons oil

250 ml/8 fl oz (1 cup) vegetable
   stock (broth)

250 ml/8 fl oz (1 cup) milk

1 tablespoon butter

freshly ground nutmeg

150 ml/5 fl oz (⅝ cup) cream

2 tablespoons thickening agent
   (such as cornflour)

freshly ground pepper
   from the mill

100 g/3½ oz (⅞ cup) grated Gouda

2 onions

2 tablespoons clarified butter

4 slices smoked pork loin

❶ Peel the potatoes and cut in half or into four, depending on size, and boil in salted water.

❷ Cut the Savoy cabbage into four, wash, remove the stalk and damaged leaves and cut into strips. Peel the onion and chop finely and dice the bacon finely. Heat 2 tablespoons of oil in a pan, add the diced bacon and chopped onion and fry until transparent. Next add the cabbage and fry with the bacon and onion. Finally, add the vegetable stock, cover and simmer for about 10 minutes.

❸ Drain the potatoes. Heat the milk, mash the potatoes, add the butter and work it into the mashed potatoes, then add the milk and whisk until the potatoes are light and airy. Season with salt and nutmeg.

❹ Add the cream to the cabbage, bring slowly to the boil, add the thickening agent and stir until it thickens. Season with salt, pepper and nutmeg.

❺ Grease a gratin dish with the rest of the olive oil and line the bottom with half the mashed potatoes. Arrange the cabbage on top, then cover with the rest of the mashed potatoes. Sprinkle with cheese.

❻ Preheat the oven to 200°C (400°F), Gas mark 6 and cook on the second shelf from the top for about 20 minutes.

❼ Peel the onions, cut into thin rings and fry in the hot clarified butter until crisp. Remove them from the pan and fry the slices of pork loin in the same fat, making sure that they are ready at the same time as the gratin. Garnish with the onion rings and serve with the fried pork loin.

Serves 4. About 1060 kcal per serving.

Gherkin gratin

It is best to use gherkins rather than cucumbers for this dish because ordinary salad cucumbers are too watery for the purpose. The roast veal can be replaced by fish such as salmon.

1 Peel the gherkins, cut into half lengthways and remove the seeds. Heat the oil in a pan, add the gherkins and fry gently for about 5 minutes on both sides. Sprinkle with lemon juice, season with salt and pepper. Wash the potatoes, boil in their skins and leave to cool.

2 Peel the potatoes, cut into thin slices and arrange in a buttered gratin dish. Arrange the gherkin halves on top and place the roast veal in the hollows.

3 Stir the cornflour into the cream together with the eggs. Season with salt and pepper. Wash the dill, pat dry, chop finely and add to the cream and egg mixture, then pour this over the gherkins.

4 Preheat the oven to 180°C (350°F), Gas mark 4 and bake on the middle shelf for about 30 minutes.

Serves 4. About 800 kcal per serving.

4 small gherkins

2 tablespoons oil

juice of ½ lemon

salt

freshly ground pepper from the mill

500 g/18 oz potatoes

1 tablespoon butter

500 g/18 oz roast veal

250 ml/8 fl oz (1 cup) cream

2 tablespoons thickening agent (such as cornflour)

2 eggs

1 bunch dill

Carrot and potato soufflé

This vegetable soufflé is not difficult to make and will delight the whole family as a light meal. It is important not to open the oven door during the cooking process or the soufflé may collapse.

1 Top and tail the carrots, peel, cut into slices and braise in a little water until soft. Wash the potatoes, boil until floury, leave to cool and peel. Push with the carrots through a potato press.

2 Generously butter a high-sided, round gratin dish. Separate the eggs, stir the egg yolks into the crème fraîche, add the chervil and stir into the carrot and potato mixture. Season with salt, pepper and nutmeg.

3 Beat the egg whites until stiff and carefully spoon over the carrot and potato mixture. Sprinkle with cheese and fold in the egg whites using a spatula.

4 Preheat the oven to 220°C (425°F), Gas mark 7 and bake on the middle shelf for about for about 30 minutes. Serve immediately.

Serves 4. About 495 kcal per serving.

300 g/10 oz carrots

300 g/10 oz potatoes

60 g/2 oz (4 tablespoons) butter

4 eggs

150 ml/5 fl oz (⅝ cup) crème fraîche

2 tablespoons chopped chervil

salt

freshly ground pepper from the mill

freshly ground nutmeg

75 g/3 oz (¾ cup) freshly grated Parmesan

Black salsify gratin

Black salsify is also known as scorzonera. As an alternative to serving it in a béchamel sauce, it can also be fried in olive oil before being arranged in the gratin dish. In this case, more cheese should be used for the gratin.

750 g/1½ lb black salsify

4 tablespoons vinegar

salt

1 pinch sugar

500 g/18 oz potatoes

30 g/1 oz (2 tablespoons) butter

30 g/1 oz (¼ cup) flour

200 ml/7 fl oz (⅞ cup) vegetable stock (broth)

200 ml/7 fl oz (⅞ cup) cream

freshly ground pepper from the mill

freshly ground nutmeg

2 tablespoons chopped parsley

100 g/3½ oz (⅞ cup) freshly grated Parmesan

❶ Peel the salsify and place immediately in cold water and vinegar to keep it white. Bring salted water with 1 tablespoon of vinegar to the boil. Cut the salsify in half, add to the boiling water and cook for about 20 minutes. Remove from the pan and drain. Wash the potatoes, cook and leave to drain.

❷ Peel the potatoes and cut into thin slices. Arrange the potato slices in a shallow gratin dish and season with salt and pepper.

❸ To make the sauce, melt butter in a small pan until it begins to foam, stir in the flour and gradually add the vegetable stock, stirring all the time. Next add the cream and simmer for another 5 minutes. Season with salt, pepper and nutmeg and stir in the parsley and half the Parmesan.

❹ Arrange the salsify on top and pour the sauce over it. Sprinkle with the rest of the cheese.

❺ Preheat the oven to 200°C (400°F), Gas mark 6. and bake on the middle shelf for about 20 minutes.

Serves 4. About 380 kcal per serving.

Asparagus gratin

Instead of the traditional way with asparagus, try this asparagus gratin. Served with potatoes and parsley and smoked salmon, it becomes a real gourmet meal. An asparagus kettle is narrow and tall, so that the spears are cooked upright with the tips being steamed. An ordinary deep saucepan can be used in the same way if the spears are tied together as a loose bunch.

1 Peel the white asparagus and cut off the woody ends. Only peel the bottom third of the green asparagus. Bring water to the boil in an asparagus kettle or deep saucepan. Add salt, sugar and half the butter. Add the asparagus, standing it vertically with the tips out of the water. Cook for about 10 minutes until "al dente". Remove from the pan and drain.

2 Remove the stalk and seeds of the peppers, wash and cut into small cubes.

3 Grease a shallow gratin dish with the rest of the butter and arrange the asparagus in it.

4 Add the eggs to the cream and whisk vigorously. Cut the cheese into small cubes. Next add the diced cheese and peppers to the egg and cream mixture. Season generously with salt and pepper and pour over the asparagus.

5 Preheat the oven to 220°C (425°F), Gas mark 7 and bake on the middle shelf for about 20 minutes.

Serves 4. About 355 kcal per serving.

500 g/18 oz white asparagus

500 g/18 oz green asparagus

salt

1 pinch sugar

20 g/3/4 oz (1½ tablespoons) butter

1 sweet red pepper

1 sweet green pepper

4 eggs

50 ml/1½ fl oz (3 tablespoons) cream

150 g/5 oz mild hard cheese

freshly ground pepper from the mill

Baked haricot beans

Baked beans are very popular in Central America and North America where they are prepared in many ways. They are delicious with fried pork chops or fried eggs as well as with baked potatoes. If the beans look as if they are becoming too dry, add a little liquid.

500 g/18 oz dried white haricot beans

salt

250 g/9 oz slices bacon

50 ml/1½ fl oz (3 tablespoons) maple syrup

3 tablespoons tomato ketchup

2 teaspoons powdered mustard

1 tablespoon balsamic vinegar

1 onion

1 pinch cayenne pepper

1 Leave the haricots beans to soak overnight in cold water. The following day, add a little salt to the water, bring to the boil, simmer for 1 hour and drain.

2 Line the bottom of a gratin dish with half the bacon slices and add the beans.

3 Make a sauce with the maple syrup, ketchup, mustard powder and balsamic vinegar. Peel the onion, chop finely and add to the sauce. Season with cayenne pepper and pour over the beans.

4 Garnish the top with the rest of the bacon. preheat the oven to 200°C (400°F), Gas mark 6 and bake on the second shelf from the bottom for about 50 minutes.

Serves 4. About 575 kcal per serving.

Cauliflower gratin

In this dish the cauliflower is cut into thick slices and flavoured with saffron, which gives it a beautiful yellow colour. With the red and green peppers and peas, this a very colourful dish. If intended for children, reduce the amount of spices used. It is delicious served with a green salad and pitta bread.

❶ Remove the leaves from the cauliflower as well as the thick stalk. Cut the whole cauliflower into finger-thick slices using a sharp knife. Bring plenty of salted water to the boil in a large pan, add a little saffron and the slices of cauliflower and boil for 6–8 minutes. It should still be very crunchy. Remove the cauliflower and drain on kitchen paper.

❷ Wash the peppers, remove the stalk, cut in half and remove the seeds. Dice the peppers very small and mix with the frozen peas. Peel the onion and chop finely.

❸ Melt 20 g/¾ oz butter in a pan, add the chopped onions and fry over low heat until soft. Add the cream and remaining saffron and simmer for a little longer. Season generously with salt, cayenne pepper, nutmeg and lemon juice, remove from the heat and leave to cool for a little.

❹ Grease a gratin dish with the remaining butter and arrange alternate layers of cauliflower slices and the peppers and peas mixture.

❺ Beat the eggs and add to the cream sauce mixture. Pour over the vegetables and sprinkle with cheese.

❻ Preheat the oven to 200°C (400°F), Gas mark 6 and bake on the second shelf from the bottom for about 25 minutes.

Serves 4. About 560 kcal per serving.

1 cauliflower
1 tablespoon saffron threads
1 sweet red pepper
1 sweet yellow pepper
300 g/10 oz frozen peas
1 onion
30 g/1 oz (2 tablespoons) butter
300 ml/10 fl oz (1¼ cups) cream
salt
1 pinch cayenne pepper
freshly ground nutmeg
1 tablespoon lemon juice
4 eggs
100 g/3½ oz mature hard cheese

500 g/18 oz fresh spinach

salt

100 g/3½ oz (⅞ cup) soft wheat flour

2 eggs

2 tablespoons sunflower seeds

4 tablespoons oil

250 g/9 oz mushrooms

1 onion

1 clove garlic

2 tablespoons olive oil

150 ml/5 fl oz (⅝ cup) cream

freshly ground pepper from the mill

2 balls mozzarella

Pancakes with spinach and mushrooms

These delicious pancakes are filled with spinach and mushrooms. But as a change they can also be filled with other vegetables, perhaps with smoked salmon.

❶ Trim the spinach and wash carefully. Cook in a small amount of salted water with the lid on, until it collapses. Remove the spinach from the pan and drain.

❷ Make a pancake batter using flour, eggs, 250 ml/8 fl oz (1 cup) water, sunflower seeds and a pinch of salt. Leave to stand for 10 minutes. Heat the oil in a non-stick frying-pan, letting it become very hot. Then make 8 pancakes.

❸ Wipe the mushrooms clean with kitchen paper and cut into very thin slices. Peel the onion and shop finely. Peel the cloves of garlic and crush in a garlic press. Heat the olive oil in a non-stick pan, add the onion and garlic and fry until transparent. Add the mushrooms and continue frying. Stir in the cream and season generously with salt and pepper. Remove from the heat.

❹ Mix one-third of the mushroom sauce with the coarsely chopped spinach and stuff the pancakes. Arrange the pancakes in a shallow gratin dish and pour the rest of the sauce on top. Cut the mozzarella into thin slices and put on top.

❺ Preheat the oven to 180°C (350°F), Gas mark 4 and bake on the middle shelf for about 20 minutes.

Serves 4. About 590 kcal per serving.

Exotic lentil gratin with curry

Lentils are prepared in many ways in India and this is a delicious example. This gratin can also be adapted to vegetarian cuisine by replacing the meat with two carrots. It is delicious served with rice and poppadoms, accompanied by a yoghourt sauce flavoured with mint that counteracts the spiciness.

250 g/9 oz red lentils

4 beef tomatoes

250 g/9 oz turkey breast escalopes

100 g/3½ oz dried apricots

2 sweet yellow peppers

2 onions

1 clove garlic

2 tablespoons clarified butter

1 tablespoon curry powder

2 teaspoons turmeric

salt

1 pinch chilli powder

3 eggs

200 g/7 oz sour cream

2 tablespoons desiccated (shredded) coconut

1 Rinse the lentils in a sieve and bring to the boil in about 1 litre/1¾ pints (4½ cups) of water. Cook over a low flame for about 8 to 10 minutes until they have absorbed sufficient water but still have some bite. Drain.

2 Make a cross-shaped cut in the tomatoes, blanch in boiling water and peel. Cut them into quarters, remove the seeds and cut into large cubes.

3 Cut the turkey meat into thin strips and the apricots into small cubes. Wash the peppers, remove the stalk and seeds and cut into narrow strips. Peel the onions and chop finely. Peel the cloves of garlic and crush with a garlic press.

4 Heat the clarified butter in a non-stick pan. Add the chopped onions and crushed garlic until transparent. Next add the turkey and peppers and fry vigorously. Sprinkle the curry and turmeric in the pan and continue frying. Added the diced tomatoes and apricots and simmer over a low heat for about 5 more minutes. Add the lentils and season generously with salt and chilli.

5 Mix together the sour cream and eggs and season with salt. Pour the lentil mixture in a shallow gratin dish, pour the sour cream and egg sauce on top and sprinkle with the desiccated (shredded) coconut . Preheat the oven to the 180°C (350°F), Gas mark 4 and bake on the middle shelf for 15–20 minutes.

Serves 4. About 620 kcal per serving.

Tasty lentil gratin

This nourishing gratin is delicious served with spicy sausages or boiled beef. Left-over vegetables may also be added.

1 Put the lentils in a saucepan with plenty of water, cover, bring to the boil and simmer for about 30 minutes.

2 Peel the potatoes and cut them cubes of 1 cm/⅜ in. Add to the lentils and simmer for a further 15 minutes. Pour away the water and drain.

3 Top and tail the carrots, celery and leeks and wash them carefully. Cut the carrots and celery into cubes and the leeks in rings. Heat some oil in a pan, add the carrots, celery and leeks and fry until golden. Next add a little water and simmer over low heat until soft.

4 Mix the vegetables with the potatoes and lentils and season generously with salt, pepper and vinegar.

5 Place in a gratin dish, cover with crème fraîche and sprinkle with cheese.

6 Preheat the oven to 220°C (425°F), Gas mark 7 and bake on the second shelf from the top for about 15 minutes.

Serves 4. About 760 kcal per serving.

300 g/10 oz large lentils

500 g/18 oz potatoes, cooked until still firm

4 carrots

¼ head celery

2 leeks

2 tablespoons oil

salt

freshly ground pepper from the mill

balsamic vinegar

200 ml/7 fl oz (⅞ cup) crème fraîche

100 g/3½ oz (⅞ cup) freshly grated Emmental

Grilled stuffed mushrooms

Giant mushrooms are ideal for stuffing and taste delicious with spinach. Stuffed mushrooms look very attractive and are an ideal starter to a meal with several courses. But it can also be served as a main meal with potato purée and a salad.

1 Pull off the stalks from the mushroom caps and wipe both caps and stalks with kitchen paper. Chop the stalks finely. Wash the spinach thoroughly and discard damaged leaves. Drain thoroughly and dry in a salad spinner. Chop up if necessary. Cut the dried tomatoes and ham into small pieces. Make breadcrumbs in a liquidizer or food processor.

2 Heat two tablespoons of olive oil in a pan, add the chopped shallot and garlic and fry until transparent. Add the spinach and cover briefly so that the spinach collapses. Then add all the remaining ingredients and fry briefly. Season with salt and pepper.

3 Put a small amount of spinach mixture in the mushroom caps and sprinkle with cheese.

4 Grease a gratin dish with the rest of the oil, arrange in the gratin dish and add the vegetable stock.

5 Preheat the oven to 200°C (400°F), Gas mark 6 and bake on the second shelf from the top for about 20 minutes.

Serves 4. About 265 kcal per serving.

8 large mushrooms

500 g/18 oz fresh spinach

2 tablespoons dried tomatoes in oil

100 g/3½ oz ham

2 slices bread for toasting

1 shallot

1 clove garlic

3 tablespoons olive oil

salt

freshly ground pepper from the mill

100 g/3½ oz (½ cup) goat's cheese

100 ml/3½ fl oz (½ cup) vegetable stock (broth)

Haricot bean gratin

When time is short, canned haricot beans can be used instead of dried ones and the sausages maybe replaced by fried diced bacon or left-over roast meat.

1 Soak the beans overnight in cold water. Wash the thyme and pat dry. Cook the beans in salted water with 1 tablespoon of oil and a sprig of thyme over low heat until tender.

2 Wash the carrots and celery sticks, trim and cut into small cubes. Peel the onion and chop finely. Heat the oil in a pan, add the chopped onion and diced vegetables and fry over medium heat for about 5 minutes. Drain the beans and add to the vegetable mixture.

3 Cut the sausages into slices and add to the beans. Season with salt and pepper. Mix the sour cream and eggs together, add the parsley and season with salt and pepper.

4 Put the bean mixture in a greased gratin dish and pour the egg and cream mixture over the top. Sprinkle with cheese. Preheat the oven to 200°C (400°F), Gas mark 6 and bake on the second shelf from the top for about 20 minutes until golden brown.

Serves 4. About 780 kcal per serving.

200 g/7 oz haricot beans

1 sprig thyme

salt

3 tablespoons olive oil

2 carrots

4 sticks celery

1 onion

4 bockwurst sausages

200 ml/7 fl oz (⅞ cup) sour cream

2 eggs

freshly ground pepper
from the mill

1 tablespoon dried parsley

75 g/3 oz (¾ cup) freshly grated
pecorino

Vegetable bake with ricotta

❶ Peel the potatoes, carrots and kohlrabi and cut into thin slices. Wash the courgettes, top and tail. Cut in half lengthways and slice thinly. Butter a gratin dish with butter and arrange the vegetables in layers, seasoning each layer with salt, pepper and nutmeg. Sprinkle with the herbs and sunflower seeds.

❷ Mix together the vegetable stock and cream and pour over the vegetables. Preheat the oven to 200°C (400°F), Gas mark 6 and bake on the middle shelf for about 40 minutes.

❸ Separate the eggs. Mix together the egg yolks and ricotta. Season with salt, pepper and nutmeg. Whisk the egg whites until they form stiff peaks and fold carefully into the quark.

❹ Increase the oven temperature to 220°C (425°F), Gas mark 7. Take the vegetables out of the oven and cover with quark mixture. Return to the oven and bake for a further 10–15 minutes until golden brown.

Serves 4. About 405 kcal per serving.

2 carrots

500 g/18 oz potatoes

1 kohlrabi

2 small courgettes (zucchini)

1 tablespoon butter

salt

freshly ground pepper
   from the mill

2 tablespoons chopped chervil
   or parsley

2 tablespoons sunflower seeds

200 ml/7 fl oz (⅞ cup) vegetable
   stock (broth)

200 ml/7 fl oz (⅞ cup) cream

3 eggs

200 g/7 oz ricotta

freshly ground nutmeg

Pumpkin casserole with leek sauce

❶ Remove the pumpkin flesh. Wash and peel the potatoes. Slice the pumpkin flesh and potatoes. Season with salt and pepper. Cover and set aside. Peel the garlic and onions. Crush the garlic and finely chop the onions. Heat the sunflower oil in a pan and sweat the onions and garlic until transparent.

❷ Turn the pumpkin and potato slices in flour. Heat olive oil in a pan and fry the pumpkin and potato slices briefly on both sides. Roughly crumble the cheese. Butter a casserole dish and put in half the pumpkin and potato slices. Spread the onion and garlic over it, distribute half the cheese over it and cover with the remaining pumpkin and potato slices. Finally scatter the remaining cheese over all.

❸ Mix the egg and cream. Season with salt, pepper and nutmeg. Wash the parsley, pat dry and finely chop the leaves. Stir the parsley into the eggs and pour over the casserole. Cook on the middle shelf of the oven preheated to 200°C (400°F), Gas mark 6 for about 40 minutes.

Serves 4. About 700 kcal per serving.

1 kg/2¼ lb pumpkin

500 g/18 oz potatoes

salt

freshly ground white pepper
   from the mill

1 clove garlic

2 onions

3 tablespoons sunflower oil

4 tablespoons flour

3 tablespoons olive oil

400 g/14 oz feta (ewes' milk)
   cheese

butter for the dish

2 eggs

125 ml/4 fl oz (½ cup) cream

freshly ground nutmeg

1 bunch flat-leaved parsley

Chinese cabbage gratin

Chinese cabbage is usually served as a salad but it is also delicious cooked. An alternative dish could use rice instead of potatoes and curry instead of paprika.

1 Chinese cabbage

150 g/5 oz bacon

250 g/9 oz turkey breast escalopes

2 tablespoons oil

1 tablespoon paprika

salt

freshly ground pepper from the mill

500 g/18 oz potatoes

200 ml/7 fl oz (⅞ cup) sour cream

200 ml/7 fl oz (⅞ cup) cream

1 egg

100 g/31/2 oz (⅞ cup) grated mild hard cheese

❶ Cut the Chinese cabbage lengthways into eight pieces, wash, remove the stalk and drain well.

❷ Cut the bacon into strips and fry until crisp in a non-stick pan. Remove from the pan and drain on kitchen paper. Cut the turkey into thin strips , add 1 tablespoon of oil to the remaining cooking fat and fry the meat in it. Sprinkle with paprika, fry briefly and season with salt and pepper. Remove from the pan. Wash the potatoes, boil in their skins and leave to cool.

❸ Add the remaining oil to the pan and fry the Chinese cabbage. Then add 50 ml/1½ fl oz (3 tablespoons) water, cover and braise for about 5 minutes.

❹ Peel the potatoes, cut into thin slices and arrange in a shallow gratin dish. Season with salt and pepper. Arrange the fried cabbage on top.

❺ Return the meat to the pan and increase the temperature. Add the cream and sour cream. Cook briefly to thicken. Season with salt and pepper.

❻ Arrange the meat on top of the fried Chinese cabbage, pour the sauce over it and sprinkle with cheese. Preheat the oven to 200°C (400°F), Gas mark 6 and bake on the middle shelf for about 25 minutes.

Serves 4. About 680 kcal per serving.

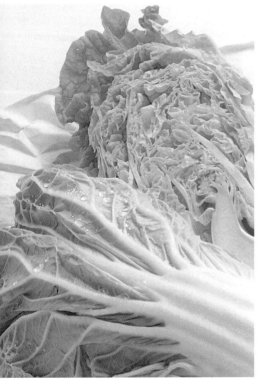

Cabbage gratin

Beneath the mouth-watering crusty cheese topping is an interesting curried cream sauce, flavoured with orange, an unusual variation on the traditional recipe with bacon.

❶ Clean the cabbage, wash, remove the stalk and cut into large strips. Peel the potatoes and cut into thin slices. Boil in salted water for 5 minutes and drain.

❷ Heat 2 tablespoons of oil in a pan. Wash the turkey meat, wipe dry, cut into thin strips and fry briskly in the hot oil. Sprinkle with curry powder and fry briefly. Next add the orange juice and vegetable stock and simmer gently for 5 minutes. Remove the meat from the sauce and leave the sauce to cool a little.

❸ Grease a shallow gratin dish with 1 tablespoon of oil and arrange alternate layers of potato slices, cabbage and turkey.

❹ Mix the cream and eggs together and stir into the cooking juices. Season generously with orange zest, salt and pepper. Pour the sauce over the gratin and sprinkle with cheese.

❺ Preheat the oven and bake on the second shelf from the bottom for about 40 minutes.

Serves 6. About 544 kcal per serving.

1 cabbage, about 1 kg/2¼ lb

600 g/1¼ lb potatoes

salt

3 tablespoons oil

600 g/1¼ lb turkey breast escalopes, cut into fine strips

1 tablespoon curry powder

juice and zest of 1 untreated orange

100 ml/3½ fl oz (½ cup) vegetable stock (broth)

300 ml/10 fl oz (1¼ cups) cream

4 eggs

freshly ground pepper from the mill

150 g/5 oz mild hard cheese

Vegetable gratin with rolled oats topping

This gratin is delicious with flash-fried meat or as a main dish with a salad. It looks particular attractive served in small ramekins.

100 g/3½ oz (2 cups) rolled oats

150 ml/5 fl oz (⅝ cup) vegetable stock (broth)

4 carrots

4 small courgettes (zucchini)

300 g/10 oz oyster mushrooms

4 tablespoons olive oil

2 shallots

1 clove garlic

1 egg

50 ml/1½ fl oz (3 tablespoons) cream

100 g/3½ oz (⅞ cup) freshly grated Parmesan

2 tablespoons pumpkin seeds

salt

freshly ground pepper from the mill

freshly ground nutmeg

½ bunch parsley

❶ Bring the vegetable stock to the boil in a pan, add the rolled oats, cover and simmer over low heat for about 30 minutes.

❷ Peel the carrots, cut in half and then into narrow strips. Wash the courgettes, top and tail and cut also into narrow strips. Wipe the mushrooms clean with kitchen paper, trim and cut into wide strips.

❸ Heat 2 tablespoons of oil in a non-stick pan, add the vegetables, fry until golden and remove from the pan. Peel the shallots and chop finely. Peel the cloves of garlic and crush in the garlic press.

❹ Heat the remaining oil in the pan, add the shallots and garlic and fry until transparent over a low heat. Mix the egg, cream, Parmesan and pumpkin seeds together with the onion and garlic mixture and season generously with salt, pepper and nutmeg.

❺ Put the vegetables in a gratin dish and cover with the rolled oats mixture. Preheat the oven to 200°C (400°F), Gas mark 6 and bake on the second shelf from the top for about25 minutes until golden brown. Wash the parsley and pat dry. Remove the leaves from the stems, chop finely and sprinkle on the gratin.

Serves 4. About 430 kcal per serving.

Garlic gratin

This gratin a true gourmet dish for all garlic lovers. It is best to use young cloves, which are milder in taste.

1 fresh bulb garlic

100 ml/3½ fl oz (½ cup) cream

100 ml/3½ fl oz (½ cup) crème fraîche

100 ml/3½ fl oz (½ cup) vegetable stock (broth)

salt

freshly ground pepper

300 g/10 oz macaroni

200 ml/7 fl oz (⅞ cup) oyster mushrooms

2 small courgettes (zucchini)

2 tablespoons olive oil

100 g/3½ oz freshly grated Gruyère

❶ Peel the garlic and cut into thin slices. Add to the cream, crème fraîche and vegetable stock. Simmer all for about 7 minutes, then purée with a hand mixer. Season with salt and pepper.

❷ Cook the macaroni in plenty of salted water until "al dente". Pour away the water, run under cold water and drain.

❸ Wipe the oyster mushrooms with kitchen paper and cut into slices. Wash the courgettes, top and tail them and grate coarsely with a vegetable grater. Fry briskly in hot olive oil and season with salt and pepper.

❹ Stir together the macaroni, garlic sauce and vegetables and spoon into a gratin dish. Sprinkle with cheese, preheat the oven to 200°C (400°F), Gas mark 6 and bake on the second shelf from the top for about 25 minutes.

Serves 4. About 560 kcal per serving.

Tomato gratin

It is important to buy good quality, waxy potatoes and ripe tomatoes. The addition of tofu makes this gratin a nourishing dish that can also be served with grilled meat and fish.

❶ Cook the potatoes in their skins, drain and leave to cool. Make a cross-shaped cut in the tomatoes , blanch in boiling water and peel. Cut the tomatoes into quarters, remove the stalks and seeds and cut into slices. Shell the hard-boiled (hard-cooked) eggs and cut into slices.

❷ Grease a gratin dish with oil. Peel the potatoes and cut into slices. Arrange the potato slices together with the tomato slices and sliced eggs so that they overlap. Season with salt and pepper.

❸ Purée the tofu with the cream in a blender. Stir in two-thirds of the Parmesan. Season with salt and pepper. Pour this mixture over the vegetables and sprinkle with the rest of the cheese and sunflower seeds.

❹ Preheat the oven to 200°C (400°F), Gas mark 6 and bake on the second shelf from the top for about 30 minutes until golden brown.

Serves 4. About 610 kcal per serving.

1 kg/2¼ lb potatoes, cooked until still firm

6 beef tomatoes

4 hard boiled (hard cooked) eggs

1 tablespoon oil

salt

freshly ground pepper from the mill

200 g/7 oz tofu with herbs

200 ml/7 fl oz (⅞ cup) cream

75 g/3 oz (¾ cup) freshly grated Parmesan

2 tablespoons sunflower seeds

Sauerkraut gratin with schupfnudeln

Schupfnudeln are a German speciality similar to gnocchi. Traditionally served with sauerkraut, here they are prepared as a gratin, made even more nourishing by the addition of sausage meat. A can of ready-cooked sauerkraut may be used instead of raw sauerkraut. Choose a mild or sharp cheese according to taste.

1 kg/2¼ lb potatoes boiled in their skins until floury the day before

salt

½ teaspoon ground nutmeg

1 egg

150 g/5 oz flour

75 g/3 oz streaky bacon

2 onions

500 g/18 oz pork sausage meat

750 g/1½ lb raw sauerkraut

1 tablespoon dried marjoram

1 tablespoon paprika

salt

freshly ground pepper from the mill

200 ml/7 fl oz (⅞ cup) cream

200 ml/7 fl oz (⅞ cup) sour cream

1 tablespoon butter

200 g/7 oz hard cheese, grated

❶ To make the *schupfnudeln*, peel the potatoes and mash in a bowl. Mix with salt, nutmeg, egg and flour to make a firm dough.

❷ Put the dough on a floured surface. Roll into lengths with a diameter of barely 1 cm/⅜ in. Cut into pieces about 4cm/1½ in long.

❸ Bring plenty of salted water to the boil in a large pan. Add the schupfnudeln and cook for 10 minutes in the boiling water so that they keep moving. Remove with a skimmer and drain well.

❹ Cut the bacon into small cubes and fry in a non-stick frying-pan until crisp. Remove from the pan. Peel the onions, chop finely, add to the pan and fry in the remaining cooking fat until transparent. Add the sausage meat and fry for about 5 minutes. Chop the sauerkraut coarsely, add to the sausage meat and fry for another 5 minutes. Season generously with marjoram, paprika, salt and pepper.

❺ Mix together the cream and the sour cream, seasoning with salt and pepper. Butter a gratin dish and arrange alternate layers of the *schupfnudeln*, three-quarters of the grated cheese and the sausage meat mixture.

❻ Finally pour the cream and sour cream mixture over the gratin. Preheat the oven to 200°C (400°F), Gas mark 6 and bake on the middle shelf for about 20 minutes. Sprinkle the rest of the grated cheese on top and return to the oven for another 10 minutes until the cheese turns golden brown.

Serves 4. About 1160 kcal per serving.

Baked beans

This delicious American bean dish is particularly good with a slice of fresh wholemeal (wholewheat) bread.

❶ Put the beans in a bowl and cover with cold water and soak for 12 hours. Pour away the water. Cover the beans with fresh water in a pan and bring to the boil. Reduce the heat and simmer for 1 hour 30 minutes. Drain the water.

❷ Dice the bacon. Peel and finely chop the onion and garlic. Cut the chilli in half. Remove and discard the core and seeds. Cut the chilli into fine strips.

❸ Heat the oil in a pan and fry the bacon until crisp. Add the onion, garlic and chilli and cook gently together for 5 minutes. Add the beans, green coriander and vegetable stock (broth). Season with salt and cayenne pepper. Cook the bean mixture for a further 5 minutes.

❹ Take the pan from the stove. Stir two-thirds of the grated Cheddar cheese into the beans. Put the beans in an oven dish and sprinkle with the remaining cheese. Preheat the oven to 200°C (400°F), Gas mark 6 and bake for 15 minutes.

Serves 4. About 620 kcal per serving.

400 g/14 oz (2¼ cups) kidney beans

80 g/3 oz bacon

1 onion

1 clove garlic

1 green chilli

1 tablespoon sunflower oil

2 tablespoons chopped coriander leaves

80 ml vegetable stock (broth)

salt

cayenne pepper

120 g/4 oz grated Cheddar cheese

Ratatouille gratin

This Provençal vegetable dish is delicious with grilled meat or a gigot of lamb. It is also an ideal dish for vegetarians, served with salad and fresh white bread. On hot days, it is also excellent cold.

1 Trim and wash the peppers, courgettes (zucchini), aubergine (eggplant) and carrots. Cut the peppers in half, remove the seeds and cut into thin strips. Cut the courgettes and aubergine into cubes of about 2 cm/¾ in. Peel the carrots and cut into thin slices. Peel the onion and chop finely, peel the cloves of garlic and crush with a garlic press.

2 Heat 3 tablespoons of oil in a pan. Add the chopped onion and crushed garlic and fry until transparent. Add the aubergines and peppers and continue frying. Now add the tomato purée. Cut the tomatoes into small pieces and add to the pan together with the juice. Stir well so that all the ingredients are well mixed.

3 Wash the thyme and rosemary, pat dry and remove the leaves from the stems. Add the herbs to the vegetable mixture. Continue simmering over low heat for 10–15 minutes until the vegetables are "al dente".

4 Spoon the ratatouille into a shallow gratin dish. Cut the cheese into thin strips and dot over the ratatouille. Sprinkle with pine kernels and the rest of the olive oil.

5 Preheat the oven to 220°C (425°F), Gas mark 7 and bake on the second shelf from the top for about 15 minutes until the cheese is golden brown.

Serves 4. About 325 kcal per serving.

1 sweet red pepper

1 sweet green pepper

2 medium courgettes (zucchini)

1 medium aubergine (eggplant)

2 carrots

1 onion

2 cloves garlic

4 tablespoons olive oil

2 tablespoons tomato puree

1 small can tomatoes

2 sprigs thyme

2 sprigs rosemary

2 bay leaves

salt

freshly ground pepper
from the mill

200 g/7 oz feta (ewes' milk)
cheese

2 tablespoons pine kernels

Tomato quiche with rocket

The base of this tomato, onion, rocket, salami and ham quiche is made with a yeast dough. For the best results all the ingredients must be at room temperature, including the egg. All the ingredients should therefore be taken out of the refrigerator in good time.

1 To make the dough: sieve the flour into a bowl and make a hollow in the centre. Sprinkle in the yeast and sugar and pour in the lukewarm milk. Mix, adding the flour little by little from the edges. Stand for about 10 minutes in a warm place.

2 Add 100 g/3½ oz (½ cup) butter at room temperature, ½ teaspoon salt and the egg. Work into a dough by hand or using the kneading hook of the mixer. Sprinkle flour on the dough, cover the bowl with a tea towel and put in a warm place. The dough can be worked again when it has doubled in size. Knead the dough vigorously after it has risen. Butter a quiche dish generously.

3 Roll out the dough about 1 cm (⅜ in) thick and line the quiche dish. Prick the base with a fork. Pour 60 g/2 oz (4 tablespoons) melted butter over the base. Leave to rise in a very cool oven, 50°C/120°F, for 20–30 minutes. Remove, then pre-heat the oven to 200°C (400°F), Gas mark 6.

4 Peel the onions and divide into rings. Cut the tomatoes into four, remove the seeds and chop coarsely. Tear the rocket into bite-sized pieces and cut the salami and boiled ham into strips.

5 Put the sour cream and quark in bowl and stir into a smooth mixture. Beat in the egg yolk. Season with salt and pepper. Pour the sour cream mixture onto the base.

6 Heat the rest of the butter in a pan, add the onion rings, fry until transparent and remove. Fry the tomatoes briefly in the same butter and season with salt and pepper. Arrange the onion rings and tomato pieces in the sour cream mixture. Add the strips of salami and ham. Garnish with rocket. Bake in the oven for about 30 minutes. Serve hot or cold.

Serves 4. About 998 kcal per serving.

350 g/12 oz (3¼ cups) flour

5 g (1 teaspoon) dried yeast

½ teaspoon sugar

150 ml/5 fl oz (⅝ cup) milk, lukewarm

200 g/7 oz (1 cup) butter

salt

1 egg

butter for the mould

2 red onions

3 beef tomatoes

½ bunch rocket

50 g/2 oz salami

50 g/2 oz cooked ham

100 ml/3½ fl oz (scant ½ cup) sour cream

100 g/3½ oz quark

2 egg yolks

pepper

8 young leeks

50 g/2 oz (4 tablespoons) butter

grated zest of 1 untreated orange

salt

**freshly ground white pepper
from the mill**

8 slices cooked ham

200 ml/7 fl oz (⅞ cup) cream

2 eggs

**150 g/5 oz (1¼ cups) grated
Gouda**

Leek gratin

The quality of the ingredients is important for this simple dish. The leeks must be young and the ham should be tasty. A bottom layer of sliced boiled potatoes may be included, or the gratin can be served with mashed potatoes.

❶ Trim the leeks, remove the dark green leaves and wash thoroughly. Melt the butter in a pan until it begins to foam and fry the leeks on all sides over medium heat. Add the orange zest and season with salt and pepper. Remove the leeks from the pan and roll each one in a slice of ham. Return to the pan and fry briefly. Add 4 tablespoons of water to dilute the cooking juices and remove from the heat.

❷ Stir together the cream and eggs, season with salt and pepper and add half the grated Gouda.

❸ Arrange the leeks wrapped in ham next to each other in a shallow gratin dish and pour the cooking juices from the pan over them. Pour the cream and egg mixture on top and sprinkle with the rest of the cheese.

❹ Preheat the oven to 200°C (400°F), Gas mark 6 and bake on the second shelf from the top for about 20 minutes until golden brown.

Serves 4. About 430 kcal per serving.

Potatoes with Peppers

A substantial, savoury potato gratin with a really special aroma. The under-layer consists of the almost-soft braised peppers with their own pleasant mild taste. On it are the potatoes and strongly spicy chillies.

1 Bake the sweet red pepper in the oven preheated to 220°C (425°F), Gas mark 7, until the skin begins to bubble. Put the pepper under a damp cloth or in a plastic bag and leave it to steam up. Peel off the skin, cut the pepper in half and remove the seeds and dividing membranes. Cut the flesh into squares of 1 cm/⅜ in.

2 Peel and finely chop the onion and garlic. Cut the bacon into small dice. Peel the potatoes and cut into slices 3 mm/⅛ in thick. Halve the chillies, remove the seeds and cut the flesh into fine slices.

3 Heat the oil in the pan and fry the bacon until crisp. Add the onion and garlic and leave to cook for a short time. Add the squares of red pepper and tomato juice. Simmer all together on a low heat for 10–15 minutes.

4 Put the potato slices in the milk and cream. Bring to the boil, then leave to cook for a further 15 minutes. Season well with salt and the green peppercorns. Grease a fireproof dish with butter. First put the red pepper mixture in the dish, then add the potatoes with the cream sauce. Sprinkle the gratin with the thinly sliced chillies and the grated Parmesan. Dot with flakes of butter. Preheat the oven to 200°C (400°F), Gas mark 6 and cook for 20–30 minutes. Sprinkle with the chopped herbs and serve.

Serves 4. About 685 kcal per serving.

800 g/1¾ lb sweet red peppers

1 small onion

1 clove garlic

100 g/3½ oz smoked bacon

800 g/1¾ lb potatoes, cooked until still firm

2 red chilli peppers

1 tablespoon oil

125 ml/4 fl oz (½ cup) tomato juice

200 ml/7 fl oz (½ cup) milk

200 ml/7 fl oz (⅞ cup) cream

1 teaspoon salt

1 teaspoon ground green peppercorns

butter for the dish

50 g/2 oz (½ cup) freshly grated Parmesan

30 g/1 oz (2 tablespoons) butter in flakes

1 tablespoon chopped herbs (parsley, basil)

Baked
pasta dishes

Tortellini gratin with sage and bacon

Pancetta is a type of Italian bacon with a distinctive flavour. But other types of bacon and different green vegetables may be used.

2 small courgettes (zucchini)

150 g/5 oz pancetta

2 tablespoons butter

20 sage leaves

500 g/18 oz tortellini with spinach and ricotta filling

salt

200 ml/7 fl oz (⅞ cup) cream

3 eggs

freshly ground pepper from the mill

freshly ground nutmeg

150 g/5 oz (1¼ cups) grated Gouda

❶ Wash the courgettes, prepare and cut into finger-thick slices. Cut the pancetta into thin strips. Melt butter in a pan, add the strips of pancetta, fry until crisp and remove from the pan.

❷ Wash the sage leaves, pat dry and fry briefly in the cooking fat. Drain on kitchen paper. Fry the sliced courgettes in the same fat.

❸ Boil the tortellini in plenty of boiling salted water until "al dente". Pour off the water and drain. Stir in the fried sage leaves, sliced courgettes and bacon. Put the pasta mixture in a greased gratin dish.

❹ Stir the eggs into the cream and season generously with salt, pepper and nutmeg. Pour over the tortellini.

❺ Sprinkle with cheese, preheat the oven to 200°C (400°F), Gas mark 6 and bake on the second shelf from the top for about 15 minutes.

Serves 4. About 940 kcal per serving.

Oriental vegetable lasagne

This is an Italian recipe with Oriental influences. The meat can be marinated overnight in the refrigerator and the vegetables prepared in advance. This makes it an easy yet impressive dish to serve when guests are invited.

❶ Cut the turkey breast escalopes into thin strips. Wash the chilli, cut in half, remove the seeds and chop finely. For the marinade, mix together the sesame oil, soya sauce, ginger, chilli pod, lime juice and honey. Stir and pour over the meat, cover and leave overnight in the refrigerator.

❷ Top and tail the carrots, peel and cut half of them into thin sticks. Cut the rest into small cubes, cook in a little water until tender and drain.

❸ Wash the spring onions and leek, prepare and cut off the dark green leaves. Cut the onions in half and the leek in rings. Wipe the mushrooms with kitchen paper, prepare and cut each into four.

❹ Purée the cooked carrots with the cream and egg yolks. Season with salt and pepper.

❺ Heat 3 tablespoons oil in a pan over high heat, fry the meat briskly and remove from the pan. Then fry the prepared vegetables in the cooking juices for about 5 minutes. Return the meat and marinade to the pan and add the vegetable stock. Simmer for 2 minutes.

❻ Grease a rectangular gratin dish with the rest of the oil and line the bottom with wan-tan pastry. Cover with one-third of the carrot purée, then one-third of the meat and vegetable mixture. Repeat these layers, finishing with a layer of carrot purée.

❼ Preheat the oven to 200°C (400°F), Gas mark 6 and bake on the middle shelf for about 20 minutes.

Serves 4. About 595 kcal per serving.

500 g/18 oz turkey breast escalopes

1 red chilli pod

1 tablespoon sesame oil

3 tablespoons dark soy sauce

1 tablespoon freshly grated ginger

juice of 1 lime

1 tablespoon honey

4 carrots

salt

1 bunch spring onions

1 leek

150 g/5 oz shitake or other mushrooms

50 ml/1½ fl oz (3 tablespoons) cream

4 egg yolks

pepper from the mill

4 tablespoons soya oil

300 ml/10 fl oz (1¼ cups) vegetable stock (broth)

200 g/7 oz sheets wan-tan pastry (from Oriental stores)

Aubergine (eggplant) noodle gratin

This lasagne made with fried slices of aubergines (eggplants) and ewe's milk cheese is extremely tasty. For more people, just increase the quantities.

4 small aubergines (eggplants)

salt

1 onion

2 cloves garlic

125 ml/4 fl oz (½ cup) olive oil

300 g/10 oz minced meat

2 tablespoons tomato puree

1 large can tomatoes

freshly ground pepper
   from the mill

1 tablespoon herbes de Provence

250 g/9 oz sheets green lasagne

400 g/14 oz feta (ewes' milk)
   cheese

1 Wash the aubergines (eggplants), remove stalk and cut lengthways into thin slices. Arrange the slices on kitchen paper and sprinkle with salt. Peel the onion and chop finely. Peel the garlic and crush in a garlic press.

2 Heat 2 tablespoons of oil in a pan, add the onions and garlic and fry until transparent. Add the minced meat and fry, then add the tomato purée, chopped tomatoes and juice and continue braising. Season with salt, pepper and herbs and simmer gently for about 15 minutes.

3 Dry the aubergines. Heat some oil in a non-stick pan and fry the aubergine slices a few at a time on both sides.

4 Pour a thin layer of sauce over the bottom of a rectangular gratin dish. Place a layer of lasagne, followed by a layer of sauce and a layer of aubergines, sprinkled with cheese. Repeat this process several times until all the ingredients have been used.

5 Preheat the oven and bake on the middle shelf for about 45 minutes until the pasta is cooked.

Serves 4. About 1000 kcal per serving.

Macaroni and courgette (zucchini) casserole

As an alternative to the courgettes (zucchini), this Italian vegetarian pasta casserole may also be made with aubergines (eggplants).

❶ Wash the tomatoes, cut a cross in the end, put in boiling water and peel. Remove stalks, cut in quarters and dice.

❷ Peel the onion and carrot, clean the celery. Wash the basil and pat dry. Remove the leaves from the stems and chop finely. Heat 2 tablespoons of oil in a pan and brown the vegetables. Add the tomatoes. Season to taste with salt, pepper and sugar. Simmer the vegetables for about 20 minutes until the mixture thickens.

❸ Clean the courgettes (zucchini) and cut crosswise into slices. Heat the remaining oil in a pan and cook the courgettes in portions until golden brown.

❹ Break the macaroni in pieces. Cook in salted boiling water until "al dente". Drain.

❺ Mix the macaroni with half the vegetable-sauce and Parmesan. Put half of this in a greased casserole and cover with the courgette slices. Cut the mozzarellas into slices and distribute half of it over the zucchini. Repeat with another layer of the remaining macaroni, courgettes and mozzarella. Pour over the remaining sauce.

❻ Cook for about 25 minutes on the second shelf of the oven preheated to 220°C (425°F), Gas mark 7.

Serves 4. About 615 kcal per serving.

500 g/18 oz tomatoes

1 onion

1 carrot

1 stick celery

½ bunch basil

4 tablespoons olive oil

salt

freshly ground pepper
  from the mill

2 pinches sugar

4 courgettes (zucchini)

250 g/9 oz macaroni

100 g/3½ oz (⅞ cup) freshly grated
  Parmesan

200 g/7 oz mozzarella

Schinkenfleckerl

This Austrian speciality also exists in different variations in Bohemia and Hungary. If it is too time-consuming to make the pasta dough, bought pasta may be used. The dish will still be delicious, but nothing tastes as good as home-made.

250 g/9 oz (2½ cups) flour

5 eggs

salt

200 g/7 oz cooked ham

100 g/3½ oz (½ cup) soft butter

freshly ground pepper
   from the mill

freshly grated nutmeg

100 ml/3½ fl oz (½ cup) sour
   cream

4 tablespoons breadcrumbs

80 g/3 oz (¾ cup) freshly grated
   Gouda

❶ Mix flour, 2 eggs, a pinch salt and some water to a smooth dough. Covers and leave for about 30 minutes.

❷ Cut the ham into small pieces. Separate the remaining eggs. Cream the yolks with 50 g/2 oz (4 tablespoons) butter, a pinch of salt, some pepper and nutmeg to taste. Mix in the sour cream. Beat the egg whites with a pinch of salt into stiff peaks.

❸ Roll out the dough to about 2 mm/$\frac{3}{32}$ in thick and leave for a short time to dry. Cut into squares 4 x 4 cm/1½ x 1½. Cook for about 4 minutes in plenty of salted boiling water. Drain.

❹ Scatter 2 tablespoons of breadcrumbs in a greased casserole dish. Mix the pasta and the ham with the egg mixture. Fold into the egg white and fill the casserole dish with the mixture. Sprinkle with cheese.

❺ Preheat the oven to 200°C (400°F), Gas mark 6. Bake on the middle shelf for 25–30 minutes.

Serves 4. About 695 kcal per serving.

150 ml/5 fl oz (⅝ cup) cream

½ teaspoon saffron threads

salt

freshly ground pepper
    from the mill

freshly ground nutmeg

300 g/10 oz tagliatelle

300 g/10 oz frozen peas

200 g/7 oz cooked shrimps

3 eggs

100 g/3½ oz (⅞ cup) freshly grated
    Parmesan

1 tablespoon butter

Tagliatelle with shrimps

This delicious tagliatelle gratin with peas and shrimps is flavoured with saffron. But other vegetables can also be used, such as carrots and cauliflower.

❶ Heat the cream, add the saffron and simmer for about 5 minutes. Season with salt, pepper and nutmeg, remove from the heat and leave to cool.

❷ Cook the tagliatelle in plenty of boiling salted water until "al dente", run under cold water and drain.

❸ Cook the peas in a small amount of salted water for about 5 minutes, drain and add to the tagliatelle together with the shrimps.

❹ Separate the eggs and stir the egg yolks into the cream. Beat the egg whites until they form stiff peaks. Add the saffron-flavoured cream to the tagliatelle, carefully fold in half the beaten egg whites and stir in half the Parmesan.

❺ Put the tagliatelle in a buttered gratin dish and sprinkle with cheese. Preheat the oven to 200°C (400°F), Gas mark 6 and bake on the middle shelf for about 40 minutes.

Serves 4. About 665 kcal per serving.

Taglierini gratin with sugar peas

It is worth choosing fresh egg pasta for this sophisticated gratin with sugar peas. In order not overpower the delicate flavour of the sugar peas, no cheese is used.

1 Top and tail the sugar peas and blanch in plenty of boiling salted water for about 4 minutes. Plunge immediately into ice-cold water so that they retain their beautiful green colour.

2 Boil the pasta in plenty of boiling salted water until it is "al dente", drain and run under cold water. Add the sugar peas to the pasta.

3 Melt the butter in a small pan until it begins to froth, add the flour, cook briefly to obtain a smooth mixture and gradually add the vegetable stock. Stir in the crème fraîche and simmer the sauce for another 5 minutes.

4 Rinse the lime under hot water, grate the zest finely and squeeze the juice. Add the lime zest and lime juice to the sauce and season with sugar, salt and pepper. Wash the chervil and chives and pat dry. Remove the leaves from the stems and chop them finely. Cut the chives into small rings. Stir the herbs into the sauce.

5 Pour the cream sauce over the pasta and sugar peas and put pasta and sugar peas in a greased gratin dish.

6 Chop the ham and bread in a food processor and sprinkle over the pasta. Dot with knobs of butter, preheat the oven and bake on the second shelf from the top for about 15 minutes.

Serves 4. About 930 kcal per serving.

1 kg/21/4 lb sugar peas

salt

400 g/14 oz taglierini

30 g/1 oz (2 tablespoons) butter

30 g/1 oz (¼ cup) flour

200 ml/7 fl oz (⅞ cup) vegetable stock (broth)

200 ml/7 fl oz (⅞ cup) crème fraîche

zest and juice of 1 untreated lime

1 pinch sugar

freshly ground white pepper from the mill

1 bunch chervil

½ bunch chives

200 g/7 oz slices mild cooked ham

4 slices bread for toasting

flakes of butter

Green lasagne with pesto

This lasagne is particularly delicious because it uses home-made pesto. Especially in summer, you can buy fresh basil with a powerful, intense aroma. If more pesto is made than is needed, the rest can be stored in a jar in the refrigerator for a couple of weeks, covered with olive oil.

1 Remove the basil leaves from the stems, wash and pat dry. Peel the garlic, crush in a garlic press, and liquidize in a blender together with the basil leaves, half the Parmesan and the pine kernels while the oil is added gradually. Season with salt and pepper.

2 To make the béchamel sauce, melt the butter in a small pan until it begins to foam, add the flour, stir and cook briefly to obtain a smooth mixture. Then add the milk and simmer gently for about 5 minutes, stirring constantly. Season with salt, pepper, nutmeg and a dash of lemon juice.

3 Cook the sheets of lasagne a few at a time in plenty of boiling salted water for about 5 minutes. Run under cold water, drain and spread out on damp kitchen paper.

4 Mix two-thirds of the béchamel sauce with the pesto and stir in a few spoonfuls of the cooking liquid. Butter a rectangular gratin dish and line the bottom with sheets of lasagne, a layer of béchamel and pesto sauce, a sprinkling of Parmesan and a few knobs of butter. Repeat this process until all the ingredients are used up.

5 Stir the rest of the Parmesan into the béchamel sauce and pour over the gratin. Dot with flakes of butter, preheat the oven to 200°C (400°F), Gas mark 6 and bake on the middle shelf for 25–30 minutes.

Serves 4. About 1275 kcal per serving.

1 large bunch basil

3 cloves garlic

175 g/6 oz (1½ cups) freshly grated Parmesan

2 tablespoons pine kernels

200 ml/7 fl oz (⅞ cup) olive oil

salt

freshly ground pepper from the mill

50 g/2 oz (4 tablespoons) butter

50 g/2 oz (½ cup) flour

500 ml/17 fl oz (2¼ cups) milk

freshly ground nutmeg

some lemon juice

500 g/18 oz green lasagne

flakes of butter

Tagliatelle gratin with herbs

This gratin is extremely quick to prepare and it is particularly tasty because of the fresh herbs. In this case it is essential to use fresh herbs (for instance a bunch of mixed herbs for the green sauce) because their aroma is much more intense than that of dried herbs.

400 g/14 oz green tagliatelle

salt

200 g/7 oz mixed herbs

30 g/1 oz (2 tablespoons) butter

4 eggs

200 ml/7 fl oz (⅞ cup) crème fraîche

freshly ground pepper from the mill

freshly ground nutmeg

150 g/5 oz (11/2 cups) grated Emmental

1 tablespoon oil

❶ Cook the tagliatelle in plenty of salted water until "al dente", run under the cold water and drain. Wash the herbs , pat dry and chop finely. Stir the herbs and butter into the tagliatelle.

❷ Separate the eggs, stir the egg yolks into the crème fraîche and season vigorously with salt, pepper and nutmeg. Add the cream and egg sauce to the tagliatelle.

❸ Beat the egg whites until they form stiff peaks and carefully fold in the tagliatelle together with the cheese.

❹ Grease the gratin dish with oil and transfer the tagliatelle into it, making sure that the top is smooth. Preheat the oven to 200°C (400°F), Gas mark 6 and bake on the middle shelf for about 40 minutes.

Serves 4. About 880 kcal per serving.

Pappardelle gratin with fennel and shrimps

The delicate aroma of the fennel combines beautifully with fish and shellfish. When buying the fennel, make sure that it really white and crisp. Try this gratin also with salmon steak cut into cubes and marinated like the shrimps.

❶ Wash the shrimps, pat dry and pour the lemon juice over them. Wash the dill, chop finely and add the shrimps. Season with salt and pepper, cover and leave to marinate.

❷ Prepare the fennel bulbs and wash them. Remove the green leaves and chop finely. Cut the fennel bulbs in half, remove the stalk and any threads there may be from the outer layer. Cut the fennel halves into slices.

❸ Heat the oil in a non-stick pan and fry the fennel slices briskly on both sides. Add the marinade, cream and white wine. Stir, cover and simmer for about 5 minutes.

❹ Cook the pappardelle in plenty of salted water until "al dente", drain in a colander, run under cold water and drain thoroughly.

❺ Remove the fennel slices from the pan, whisk the egg yolks and add to the sauce to thicken. Remove immediately from the heat so that the egg yolks do not curdle. Season with salt and pepper, add the finely chopped fennel leaves and stir in the shrimps.

❻ Add the shrimp sauce to the pappardelle. Grease a shallow gratin dish and arrange alternate layers of pappardelle and fennel slices. Sprinkle with Parmesan, preheat the oven to 200°C (400°F), Gas mark 6 and bake on the middle shelf for about 25 minutes.

Serves 4. About 670 kcal per serving.

200 g/7 oz cooked shrimps

2 tablespoons lemon juice

1 bunch dill

salt

freshly ground white pepper from the mill

2 bulbs fennel

2 tablespoons oil

250 ml/8 fl oz (1 cup) cream

50 ml/1½ fl oz (3 tablespoons) dry white wine

300 g/10 oz pappardelle

2 egg yolks

100 g/3½ oz (⅞ cup) freshly grated Parmesan

Ravioli and salami gratin

This gratin is popular both with children and adults. But it can also be made with other kinds of ravioli and vegetables.

1 sweet red pepper

1 sweet green pepper

1 onion

1 clove garlic

2 tablespoons olive oil

1 small can tomatoes

2 sprigs thyme

1 tablespoon paprika

salt

freshly ground pepper
from the mill

500 g/18 oz ravioli with cheese
filling

100 g/3½ oz slices air-dried
salami

2 balls mozzarella (250 g/9 oz)

1 tablespoon dried oregano

❶ Wash the peppers, prepare and cut into thin strips. Peel the onion and chop finely. Peel the garlic and crush.

❷ Heat the oil in a non-stick pan, add the onion and garlic and fry until transparent. Next add the peppers and fry briefly. Chop the tomatoes into small pieces and add with the tomato juice to the onion, garlic and peppers. Wash the thyme and pat dry. Remove the leaves from the stems and add to the rest of the ingredients. Season generously with paprika, salt and pepper and simmer gently for another 10 minutes.

❸ Cook the ravioli in plenty of boiling salted water until "al dente", drain, plunge in cold water and then drain again.

❹ Cut the salami into strips, stir into the pasta together with the sauce and put into a gratin dish

❺ Strain the mozzarella, cut into slices and sprinkle over the gratin. Preheat the oven to 200°C (400°F), Gas mark 6 and cook on the middle shelf for about 15 minutes.

Serves 4. About 745 kcal per serving.

Macaroni gratin with smoked fish

This gratin is very quick and easy to make and tastes particularly delicious with the addition of smoked fish.

400 g/14 oz macaroni

salt

300 g/10 oz smoked fish

4 beef tomatoes

2 eggs

200 g/7 oz cream

freshly ground pepper
 from the mill

freshly ground nutmeg

½ bunch parsley

½ bunch chives

100 g/3½ oz grated mild hard
 cheese

1 tablespoon butter

❶ Cook the macaroni in plenty of salted water until "al dente", run under cold water and drain.

❷ Remove the skin and bones of the fish, shred and stir into the macaroni.

❸ Make a cross-shaped cut in the tomatoes, blanch in boiling water and peel. Cut the tomatoes into four, remove the seeds and chop into large pieces and add to the macaroni.

❹ Stir the eggs into the cream, season generously with salt, pepper and nutmeg. Wash the parsley and chives and pat dry. Remove the leaves from the stems and chop them finely. Cut the chives into small rings. Add the herbs and half the cheese to the cream and egg mixture.

❺ Butter a gratin dish and fill with the macaroni mixture. Pour the cream sauce over it and sprinkle with the rest of the cheese.

❻ Preheat the oven and cook on the middle shelf for about 25 minutes.

Serves 4. About 745 kcal per serving.

Pasta gratin with mushrooms

This vegetarian gratin has a wonderful fragrance of mushrooms. This gratin can also be made with other kinds of mushrooms such as oyster mushrooms or chanterelles.

1 Wash the tomatoes, cut into half and remove the stalks and cut into thick slices. Heat 2 tablespoons of olive oil in a non-stick pan, add the tomato slices, fry on both sides and remove from the pan. Season with salt and pepper.

2 Wipe the field mushrooms with kitchen paper, prepare, cut into thick slices, add to the pan and fry briskly in the remaining oil. Wash the parsley, pat dry and chop the leaves coarsely. Add half the parsley to the mushrooms and season generously with salt and pepper.

3 Cook the rigatoni in plenty of boiling salted water until "al dente", drain and stir in the butter.

4 Liquidize the curd cheese, ewe's milk cheese, broken into small pieces, and the milk using a hand-mixer. Stir in the eggs and season with salt and pepper.

5 Put half the pasta in a greased gratin dish, arrange the mushroom – and tomato slices on top and cover with the rest of the pasta.

6 Pour the cheese mixture on top, preheat the oven to 200°C (400°F), Gas mark 6 and bake on the middle shelf for about 30 minutes. Sprinkle with the rest of the parsley.

Serves 4. About 745 kcal per serving.

4 large beef tomatoes

4 tablespoons olive oil

salt

freshly ground pepper from the mill

400 g/14 oz mushrooms

1 bunch flat-leaved parsley

300 g/10 oz Rigatoni

2 tablespoons butter

100 g/3½ oz curd cheese

100 g/3½ oz ewe's milk cheese (Feta)

400 ml/14 fl oz (1¾ cups) milk

4 eggs

Cannelloni with poultry filling

Although it takes some time to prepare this Italian casserole, the result is well worth the effort.

1 Peel and chop the garlic and one onion. Wash the rosemary and sage and pat dry. Remove the rosemary leaves and chop finely with the sage. Drain the canned tomatoes, reserving the juice, and roughly chop .

2 Heat 2 tablespoons of oil in a pan. Fry the onion, garlic and herbs. Add the chopped tomato and juice. Cook for about 15 minutes. Season to taste with salt, pepper and sugar.

3 For the bechamelsauce melt the butter in a pan, add the flour and stir. Add the milk little by little, stirring continuously, and bring to the boil. Stir in the Parmesan. Season with salt to taste and remove from the stove.

4 Peel the remaining onion and chop finely. Clean the mushrooms with kitchen paper and cut into small pieces. Dice the meat into 5 mm/³⁄₁₆ in cubes. Heat the remaining oil in a pan and brown the meat. Add the onion and mushrooms. Cook for about 5 minutes. Season to taste with salt, pepper and thyme. Cut the mozzarellas into small dice and stir in.

5 Pour the tomato-sauce into a greased casserole dish. Fill the canneloni with the meat and muchroom mixture, using a teaspoon or a forcing bag without a nozzle. Lay the filled canneloni on the tomato sauce. Pour the bechamel sauce over all.

6 Cook for about 40 minutes in on the middle shelf of the oven preheated to 200°C (400°F), Gas mark 6.

Serves 4. About 905 kcal per serving.

1 clove garlic, 2 onions

1 sprig rosemary

3 leaves sage

2 cans tomatoes, 400 g/14 oz each

4 tablespoons oil

salt

freshly ground pepper from the mill

1 pinch sugar

30 g/1 oz (2 tablespoons) butter

30 g/1 oz (¼ cup) flour

500 ml/17 fl oz (2¼ cups) milk

50 g/2 oz (½ cup) freshly grated Parmesan

300 g/10 oz mushrooms

400 g/14 oz turkey breast escalopes

1 tablespoon dried thyme

125 g/4½ oz mozzarella

20 cannelloni

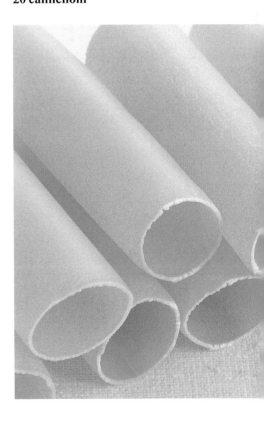

Gratiné tortellini with mushrooms

The tortellini are accompanied by a tasty mushroom sauce, made with several kinds of mushrooms. Choose tortellini with a mushroom or ricotta and spinach filling. If fontina cheese is not available, use Gruyère or a mild mountain cheese instead.

- 250 g/9 oz chanterelles
- 250 g/9 oz field mushrooms
- 250 g/9 oz oyster mushroom
- 2 shallots
- 2 cloves garlic
- 2 tablespoons olive oil
- 300 ml/10 fl oz (1¼ cups) mushroom stock (broth)
- 300 ml/10 fl oz (1¼ cups) crème fraiche
- 3 tablespoons sauce thickening
- salt
- freshly ground white pepper from the mill
- 2 tablespoons dried parsley
- 500 g/18 oz tortellini
- 100 g/3½ oz fontina cheese, sliced

❶ Wipe the chanterelles and field mushrooms with kitchen paper. Trim the mushrooms and cut the large chanterelles in half, the field mushrooms in four and the oyster mushrooms in strips. Peel the shallots and chop finely. Peel the garlic and push through the garlic press.

❷ Heat the olive oil in a non-stick pan, add the chopped shallots and garlic and fry until transparent. Next add the mushrooms and fry briskly. Stir in the mushroom stock and crème fraîche and simmer gently for about 5 minutes. Add the thickening and season with salt, pepper and parsley.

❸ Par-boil the tortellini in plenty of boiling water, drain and stir in the mushroom sauce.

❹ Arrange in four individual ramekins and sprinkle with fontina. Preheat the oven and bake on the middle shelf for about 20 minutes.

Serves 4. About 950 kcal per serving.

Asparagus lasagne with smoked salmon

Lasagne with a difference: this fine casserole will royally spoil both family and guests.

❶ Clean and trim the asparagus, keeping the peelings and ends. Cut the asparagus into pieces 4 cm/1½ in long. Put the peelings and asparagus ends in a pan in 2 litres/3 1/2 pints (9 cups) of water with 1 teaspoon of salt, sugar and 1 tablespoon of butter. Strain. Remove about 600/20 fl oz (2½ cups) of the cooking liquid and put aside. Bring the rest to the boil and blanch the asparagus pieces in it for about 5 minutes. Remove, quench in cold water and drain.

❷ Peel the onion and chop finely. Clean the mushrooms with kitchen paper rub off, clean and cut into slices. Wash the parsley and dab dry. Remove the leaves from the stalks and chop finely.

❸ Heat 1 tablespoon of butter in a pan. Cook the onions until transparent, add the mushrooms and fry for about 5 minutes. Dust with flour, add the reserved cooking liquid and cream and mix together. Bring to the boil and thicken slightly. Add parsley and season the sauce with salt and pepper to taste.

❹ Cut the salmon into thin strips. Put a layer of sauce in a greased casserole dish and cover with sheets of lasagne. On it put one-third of the asparagus and one-third of the salmon. Cover with about one-quarter of the sauce. Repeat this process until all the ingredients are used, finishing with a layer of sauce. Sprinkle on the cheese sprinkles and put the remaining butter on it in flakes.

❺ Cook for about 45 minutes on the middle shelf of the oven preheated to 200°C (400°F), Gas mark 6.

Serves 4–6. About 695 kcal per serving.

2 kg/4½ lb white asparagus

salt

1 tablespoon sugar

3 tablespoons butter

1 onion

500 g/18 oz mushrooms

1 bunch parsley

2 tablespoons flour

400 ml/14 fl oz (1¾ cups) cream

freshly ground white pepper
  from the mill

250 g/9 oz smoked salmon

250 g/9 oz lasagne

20 g/¾ oz (scant ¼ cup) freshly
  grated Parmesan

Baked potato dishes

Potato and minced meat gratin

This gratin which combines several vegetables and minced meat is also very good as a party dish because it can be made in large quantities.

❶ Boil the potatoes in their skins for 15 minutes. Peel them and cut into slices 5 mm/³⁄₁₆ in thick.

❷ Prepare the peppers, wash them and cut into thin strips. Peel the garlic and crush. Peel the onion and chop finely.

❸ Heat the oil in a non-stick pan, add the onion and garlic and fry until transparent. Next add the minced meat and fry briskly. When the meat has browned nicely, add the peppers and fry them too. Season generously with salt, pepper, paprika and herbs of Provence.

❹ Beat the eggs into the milk and season vigorously with salt, pepper and nutmeg.

❺ Grease a not too shallow gratin dish, fill with half the potato slices and cover with half the frozen peas. Arrange the minced meat and pepper mixture on top and sprinkle with half the cheese. Add the rest of the peas and cover with the remaining potato slices.

❻ Pour the milk and egg mixture on top, preheat the oven to 180°C (350°F), Gas mark 4 and bake on the middle shelf for about 35 minutes until the potatoes are soft and the cheese is golden brown.

Serves 4. About 815 kcal per serving.

750 g/1½ lb potatoes

1 sweet red pepper

1 sweet yellow pepper

1 onion

1 clove garlic

3 tablespoons olive oil

5500 g/18 oz minced meat

salt

freshly ground pepper
   from the mill

1 tablespoon paprika

1 tablespoon herbes de Provence

4 eggs

300 ml/10 fl oz (1¼ cups) milk

300 g/10 oz frozen peas

150 g/5 oz (11/4 cups) freshly
   grated Gouda

Egg and potato gratin

The addition of four eggs to this gratin makes it a very nourishing dish, delicious served with salad, fried sausages and tomato sauce.

1 Peel the potatoes and carrots, wash and prepare the courgettes, peel the onion and garlic. Grate them all finely in a food processor or by hand.

2 Mix all the vegetables together in a bowl, add the parsley and the thickening agent, stir in the cream and 1 egg and season with salt, pepper and nutmeg.

3 Butter a deep gratin dish. Put the vegetable mixture in it and smooth down the surface. Make four depressions at regular intervals. Break an egg into each and sprinkle with cheese.

4 Preheat the oven to 200°C (400°F), Gas mark 6 and bake on the middle shelf for about 30 minutes.

Serves 4. About 385 kcal per serving.

750 g/1½ lb potatoes, cooked until still firm

2 carrots

2 courgettes (zucchini)

1 onion

1 clove garlic

2 tablespoons dried parsley

1 tablespoon thickening agent

150 ml/5 fl oz (⅝ cup) cream

5 eggs

salt

freshly ground pepper from the mill

freshly ground nutmeg

1 tablespoon butter

75 g/3 oz (¾ cup) grated Gouda

1 kg/2¼ lb broccoli

salt

2 eggs

100 ml/3½ fl oz (½ cup) crème fraiche

freshly ground pepper from the mill

freshly ground nutmeg

1 sweet red pepper

1 sweet yellow pepper

2 tablespoons oil

500 g/18 oz potatoes, cooked until still firm

150 ml/5 fl oz (⅝ cup) cream

50 g/2 oz (½ cup) freshly grated Parmesan

flakes of butter

Broccoli gratin with potato topping

This colourful gratin is delicious served with meat. Instead of broccoli spinach may be used.

❶ Prepare the broccoli, wash and separate into florets. Cook in slightly salted water, then drain.

❷ Separate the eggs, beat the egg whites until they form stiff peaks and place in a cool place. Purée the crème fraîche and egg yolks together with the broccoli. Season with salt, pepper and nutmeg.

❸ Prepare the peppers, wash them, halve them and remove the seeds. Then cut into thin strips. Fry in hot oil in a non-stick pan for about 5 minutes and stir in the broccoli purée.

❹ Peel the cooked potatoes and rinse them. Slice them very thinly.

❺ Fold the stiffly beaten egg whites into the broccoli purée, pour into a greased gratin dish and level off. Arrange the potato slices on top so that they overlap. Season with salt and pepper and pour the cream over all.

❻ Preheat the oven to 200°C (400°F), Gas mark 6 and bake on the middle shelf for about 30 minutes. Sprinkle with Parmesan, dot with knobs of butter and bake again for about 15 minutes until the potatoes are done and the cheese is golden brown.

Serves 4. About 530 kcal per serving.

Potato gratin with leeks and apples

2 leeks

750 g/1½ lb potatoes

salt

freshly ground pepper
  from the mill

200 ml/7 fl oz (⅞ cup) cream

2 Bramley or other non-sweet
  apples

150 g/5 oz (1¼ cups) grated
  Gouda cheese

80 g/3 oz (¼ cup) sunflower seeds

½ teaspoon dried marjoram

2 tablespoons butter

A delicious mixture of potatoes, leeks, cheese and apples - spicy and mild at the same time. This vegetarian dish is also enjoyed by children.

❶ Clean the leek, wash and cut into thin rings. Pell the potatoes and cut into very thin slices.

❷ Put alternate layers of leek and potatoes in a greased casserole dish. Season with salt and pepper. Add the cream at the sides.

❸ Peel the apples, quarter, remove cores and cut into dice. Mix the apple with the cheese and sunflower seeds and season with pepper and marjoram. Spread over the lekk and potatoes in the dish and finish with the flakes of butter.

❹ IPreheat the oven to 200°C (400°F), Gas mark 6 and cook on the middle shelf for about 60 minutes.

Serves 4. About 560 kcal per serving.

Potato gratin with anchovy

Anchovies have a very strong taste and are very salty. Therefore, add very little salt. Smoked salmon can be used instead of the anchovies.

1 Peel the potatoes and risne. Peel the onions. Slice both very thinly and mix them together.

2 Drain the anchovies and chop the capers finely.

3 Stir together the cream and sour cream and season with salt and pepper.

4 Butter a gratin dish and arrange half the potato and onion slices in itPress to flatten the surface. Arrange the anchovies and capers on top and cover with the rest of the potato and onion slices.

5 Press down again and pour a little anchovy oil and cream over all.

6 Make the breadcrumbs in a food processor or liquidizer and sprinkle on top. Dot with a knobs of butter. Preheat the oven to 200°C (400°F), Gas mark 6 and bake on the middle shelf for about 60 minutes.

Serves 4. About 620 kcal per serving.

1 kg/2¼ lb potatoes, cooked until still firm

2 large onions

2 containers anchovies (about 60 g/2 oz)

1 tablespoon capers

250 ml/8 fl oz (1 cup) cream

250 ml/8 fl oz (1 cup) sour cream

1 tablespoon butter

salt

freshly ground pepper from the mill

2 slices bread for toasting

flakes of butter

Aubergine (eggplant) and potato gratin

This casserole is also very good with courgettes (zucchini) instead of the aubergines (eggplant). Also, instead of tomatoes, oyster mushrooms can be used.

500 g/18 oz potatoes

600 g/1¼ lb tomatoes

6 anchovy fillets from a jar

800 g/1¾ lb aubergines (eggplants)

100 g/3½ oz stoned black olives

250 g/9 oz mozzarella

300 ml/10 fl oz (1¼ cups) cream

250 ml/8 fl oz (1 cup) milk

3 eggs

100 g/3½ oz blue cheese (Roquefort or Gorgonzola)

salt

freshly ground pepper from the mill

freshly ground nutmeg

❶ Boil the potatoes for about 15 minutes. Peel and cut into slices about 3–4 mm (⅛ in)thick.

❷ Wash the tomatoes, cut a cross in the end, put in boiling water and remove the skins. Remove the stalk, cut into quarters and chop the quarters into large dice. Drain the anchovies and cut in half lengthways. Clean the aubergines (ggplants) and cut crosswise into thin slices. Halve the olives and cut the mozzarella in disks.

❸ Mix cream, milk and eggs together. Crumble the cheese and stir in, with salt, pepper and nutmeg to taste.

❹ Put consecutive layers of potatoes, tomatoes, aubergines and mozzarella in a greased casserole dish. Season with salt and peppers. Spread the olives and anchovies over it. Pour over the egg,cheese and milk mixture.

❺ Preheat the oven to 300c and cook on the middle shelf for about 25 minutes.

Serves 4. About 760 kcal per serving.

Sausage and potato gratin

This nourishing gratin with vegetables, horseradish sauce and tasty sausages is a perfect dish for a cold winter's day.

❶ Boil the potatoes in their skins until cooked, drain and peel.

❷ Peel the carrots and parsley root and slice thinly. Wash the leek and celery, prepare them and slice thinly also. Bring water to the boil and add salt, vinegar, a bay leaf and the shallot. Add the sliced vegetables, blanch for about 3 minutes and drain.

❸ To make the sauce, melt butter in a small saucepan until it begins foam, add the flour, brown lightly and stir in the milk gradually. Next add the crème fraîche and stock, stirring constantly, and simmer gently for 5 minutes. Stir in the horseradish and season generously with salt, pepper, nutmeg and lemon juice.

❹ Cut the potatoes into slices. 5 mm/³⁄₁₆ in thick

❺ Heat 1 tablespoon of oil in a non-stick pan and fry the sausages, take them out of the pan and cut into slices 1 cm/³⁄₈ in thick. Stir into the vegetables.

❻ Grease a gratin dish with the rest of the oil. Arrange half the potato slices and season with salt and pepper. Pour a little sauce on top and arrange a layer of the vegetable and sausage mixture. Cover with the rest of the potatoes and pour the rest of the sauce over all.

❼ Sprinkle with breadcrumbs and dot with knobs of butter. Preheat the oven to 200°C (400°F), Gas mark 6 and bake on the middle shelf for about 35 minutes.

Serves 4. About 845 kcal per serving.

750 g/1½ lb potatoes, cooked until still firm

2 carrots, 1 root parsley

1 leek, 4 sticks celery

salt

2 tablespoons wine vinegar

1 bay leaf, 1 shallot

20 g/¾ oz (1½ tablespoons) butter

20 g/¾ oz (3 tablespoons) flour

150 ml/5 fl oz (⅝ cup) milk

150 ml/5 fl oz (⅝ cup) crème fraîche

300 ml/10 fl oz (1¼ cups) meat stock (broth)

2 tablespoons horseradish sauce

freshly ground pepper from the mill

freshly ground nutmeg

squeeze lemon juice

2 tablespoons oil

4 spicy sausages

3 tablespoons breadcrumbs

flakes of butter

800 g/1¾ lb potatoes, cooked
    until still firm

1 clove garlic

salt

freshly ground white pepper
    from the mill

freshly ground nutmeg

500 g/18 oz cream

50 g/2 oz (½ cup) freshly grated
    Parmesan

flakes of butter

Traditional potato gratin

This classic dish combines beautifully with most meat dishes, such as roast leg of lamb. Whether to use cream only or a mixture of cream and milk is a matter of both calories and taste. Also, the cheese may be left out to reduce the calorie count.

❶ Peel the potatoes and rinse them. Slice very thinly.

❷ Grease a large, shallow gratin dish and rub with the peeled garlic. Arrange the potato slices in several layers so that they overlap. Season each layer with salt, pepper and nutmeg.

❸ Pour the cream over the potatoes, Preheat the oven to 200°C (400°F), Gas mark 6 and bake on the middle shelf for about 30 minutes. Sprinkle with Parmesan and dot a few knobs of butter on top. Return to the oven for another 15 minutes and bake until the potatoes are cooked and the cheese is golden brown.

Serves 4. About 515 kcal per serving.

Potato and courgette gratin

This variation on the traditional potato gratin, accompanied by a sumptuous salad can be served as a main course or as a side-dish with quick-fried meat. To do the dish justice, the quality of the potatoes is important, and fresh rather than long-life cream should be used.

4 small courgettes (zucchini)

750 g/1½ lb potatoes, cooked until still firm

2 sprigs thyme

1 clove garlic

1 tablespoon olive oil

salt

freshly ground pepper from the mill

freshly ground nutmeg

100 g/3½ oz cream

2 tablespoons sunflower seeds

2 tablespoons pumpkin seeds

100 g/3½ oz freshly grated pecorino

knobs of butter

❶ Wash and prepare the courgettes. Peel the potatoes and wash. Slice the potatoes and courgettes very thinly. Wash the thyme and pat dry. Remove the leaves from the stems and chop finely.

❷ Peel the garlic and cut into half. Rub a shallow gratin dish with the garlic and grease with olive oil.

❸ Arrange alternate layers of potato and courgette slices (to ensure an even consistency). Season each layer with salt, pepper and nutmeg.

❹ Pour the cream over the gratin and sprinkle with sunflower and pumpkin seeds. Preheat the oven to 180°C (350°F), Gas mark 4 and bake on the middle shelf for about 30 minutes. Sprinkle pecorino on top, dot with a few knobs of butter and bake for another 10–15 minutes until the cheese is golden brown and potatoes are done.

Serves 4. About 480 kcal per serving.

Celeriac and potato grat.

Sadly celeriac is mostly used only as an ingredient in soups. If the root
are bought in summer they may still have their leaves, which add a spicy
flavour to the dish, but they are not essential.

1 Melt the butter in a small pan until it begins to foam, add the flour and
brown lightly. Add the crème fraîche and vegetable stock and simmer for about
5 minutes, stirring constantly. Season with salt and pepper and stir in the
cheese.

2 Peel the potatoes and celeriac and slice very thinly. Wash the celery leaves
and chop finely. Wash the parsley and pat dry. Chop the parsley leaves finely
and mix with the celeriac leaves.

3 Butter a gratin dish and arrange alternate layers of potato and celeriac slices
so that they overlap. Season each layer with salt and pepper and sprinkle with
parsley and celeriac leaves.

4 Pour the sauce on top and sprinkle with sesame seeds. Preheat the oven to
200°C (400°F), Gas mark 6 and bake on the middle shelf for about 1 hour.

Serves 4. About 605 kcal per serving.

salt

**freshly ʒ
  from the**

**100 g/3½ oz (ʌ　　ρ) freshly grated
  Emmental,**

**500 g/18 oz potatoes, cooked
  until still firm**

**1 large or 2 small celeriac, with
  leaves if possible**

½ bunch parsley

1 tablespoon butter

4 tablespoons sesame seeds

Potato gratin Parmentier

It was Monsieur Parmentier, a French horticulturist, who encouraged the large-scale cultivation of potatoes in France during the 18th century. This light gratin, named after him, is delicious with meat and fish dishes but can also be served as a main course with a salad.

1 Peel the potatoes, cut into large pieces and cook in salted water until soft.

2 Separate the eggs, stir the egg yolks into the cream and season with salt, pepper and nutmeg. Beat the egg whites until they form stiff peaks.

3 Drain the cooked potatoes and push through a potato press while they are still hot.

4 Stir the butter and cheese into the mashed potatoes. Add the egg and cream mixture and whisk vigorously. Now carefully fold in the beaten egg whites.

5 Butter a shallow gratin dish and put the potato mixture in it, smooth down the surface and sprinkle with breadcrumbs. Dot with knobs of butter, preheat the oven to 200°C (400°F), Gas mark 6 and bake on the middle shelf for about 20 minutes.

Serves 4. About 735 kcal per serving.

1 kg/2¼ lb potatoes

salt

4 eggs

200 ml/7 fl oz (⅞ cup) cream

freshly ground pepper from the mill

freshly ground nutmeg

100 g/4 oz (½ cup) butter

100 g/3½ oz (⅞ cup) grated
   mountain cheese

50 g/2 oz breadcrumbs

flakes of butter

300 g/10 oz potatoes

2 bulbs fennel

4 tomatoes

600 g/1¼ lb white fish fillets

2 tablespoons lemon juice

salt

freshly ground pepper
  from the mill

200 ml/7 fl oz (⅞ cup) cream

200 ml/7 fl oz (⅞ cup) sour cream

4 egg yolks

1 bunch dill

freshly ground nutmeg

1 tablespoon butter

2 tablespoons flaked almonds

Potato and fennel gratin with fish

Fish and fennel go particularly well together. For vegetarians, the fish can be replaced with braised carrot slices and 50 g/2 oz grated cheese added to the cream.

❶ Cook the potatoes in their skins until tender, drain, plunge in cold water and peel. Cut into slices 1 cm/⅜ in thick .

❷ Remove the leaves from the fennel, wash and pat dry, chop finely and put to one side. Wash and prepare the fennel bulbs. Cut in half and remove the stalk. Cut each fennel half into four slices, blanch them for about 5 minutes and drain.

❸ Make a cross-shaped cut in the tomatoes, blanch them in boiling water and peel. Cut the tomatoes into eight pieces, remove the stalks and the seeds.

❹ Cut the fish fillets into large strips and sprinkle with lemon juice. Season with salt and pepper.

❺ Mix together the cream, sour cream and egg yolks. Season generously with salt, pepper and nutmeg. Stir in the dill and fennel leaves.

❻ Butter a gratin dish and arrange the potato slices in it. Season with salt and pepper. Arrange the fennel slices, tomato segments and strips of fish fillet in rows on top. Then pour the egg and cream mixture over all and sprinkle with almond flakes.

❼ Preheat the oven to 200°C (400°F), Gas mark 6 and bake on the middle shelf for about 30 minutes.

Serves 4. About 585 kcal per serving.

Potato and leek gratin

This gratin will appeal to the whole family. If time is short, instant mashed potato may be used.

1 Peel the potatoes, wash and cut them into pieces. Then boil them in salted water until they are soft. Drain them and push through a potato press while they are still hot. Add butter and milk and whisk into a purée. Season with salt and pepper.

2 Butter a gratin dish, put the potato purée in it and flatten the surface.

3 Prepare the leeks and cut off the dark green leaves. Cut in half lengthways, wash thoroughly and cut into pieces 3 cm/1¼ in long . Melt the remaining butter in a non-stick pan, add the leeks and fry over low heat for about 5 minutes. Season with salt and pepper.

4 Cut the ham into small cubes, stir in the leeks, then pour this over the potato purée.

5 Stir the egg into the cream, season with salt and pepper and pour it over the top of the leeks and ham.

6 Sprinkle with cheese, preheat the oven to 220°C (425°F), Gas mark 7 on the second shelf from the top for about 20 minutes.

Serves 4. About 465 kcal per serving.

600 g/1¼ lb potatoes

250 ml/8 fl oz (1 cup) milk

50 g/2 oz (4 tablespoons) butter

**freshly ground pepper
    from the mill**

2 leeks

**2 thick slices cooked ham,
    about 150 g/5 oz**

1 egg

150 ml/5 fl oz (⅝ cup) cream

75 g/3 oz (¾ cup) grated Gouda

Potato and paprika casserole

The mild creamed cheese makes this casserole a banquet for the whole family.

500 g/18 oz potatoes

salt

4 sweet yellow peppers

250 g/9 oz cherry tomatoes

300 g/10 oz pork sausages

4 eggs

200 ml/7 fl oz (⅞ cup) cream

150 g/5 oz (⅞ cup) freshly grated
 Gouda cheese

freshly grated nutmeg

freshly ground pepper
 from the mill

30 g/1 oz (2 tablespoons) butter

① Peel the potatoes peel and cut into thin slices. Blanch in about 1 litre/1¾ pints (4½ cups) boiling salted water for 3 minutes. Remove and drain. Wash the peppers, cut in half, remove the pips and membrane and cut into strips of about 3 cm/1¼ in.

② Wash the tomatoes and prick two or three times with a toothpick. Cut the sausages in dice about 1 cm/⅜ in thick.

③ Put half the potatoes into a well greased casserole dish. Add consecutive layers of half the pepper strips, sausage, tomatoes and the remaining potatoes.

④ Whisk the eggs with the cream and two-thirds of the cheese. Season to taste with nutmeg, salt and peppers tastes and pour the mixture over the casserole. Distribute the remaining pepper strips and prinkle with the rest of the cheese. Dot with flakes of butter. Cover with aluminium foil.

⑤ Preheat the oven to 220°C (425°F), Gas mark 7 and cook on the middle shelf for about 40 miutes. Remove the aluminium foil after about 20 minutes.

Serves 4. About 665 kcal per serving.

Potato and cauliflower gratin

This slightly spicy dish is very popular with children.

600 g/1¼ lb potatoes

1 cauliflower

salt

200 ml/7 fl oz (⅞ cup) cream

1 lemon

freshly ground pepper
  from the mill

4 tomatoes

100 g/3½ oz bacon

1 bunch chives

75 g/3 oz (½ cup) grated Gouda

1 Boil the potatoes, peel and cut into slices 1 cm/⅜ in thick .

2 Prepare the cauliflower, wash and separate into florets. Cook in a slightly salted water with the lid on until tender. Mash with a potato masher and stir in the cream. Season with lemon juice, salt and pepper.

3 Make a cross-shaped cut in the tomatoes, blanch in boiling water and peel. Cut the tomatoes into eight segments, remove the stalks and the seeds.

4 Cut the bacon into slices and fry in a non-stick pan until crisp.

5 Grease a gratin dish with the cooking fat from the bacon and arrange the potato slices in it. Then arrange the bacon slices and tomato segment on top. Season with salt and pepper.

6 Stir the cheese into the cauliflower purée and pour over the gratin. Preheat the oven to 200°C (400°F), Gas mark 6 and bake on the middle shelf for about 25 minutes. Wash the chives, dab dry, chop into small rings and sprinkle over the gratin.

Serves 6. About 480 kcal per serving.

Potato and cep gratin

The dried ceps give this gratin a particularly delicious aroma. It is important to use good, waxy potatoes such as Charlotte. The dish is delicious served with roast pork.

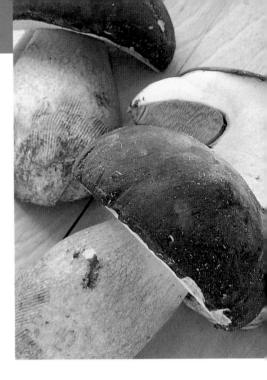

1 Soak the ceps in 250 ml/8 fl oz (1 cup) of warm water and leave to stand for at least 30 minutes. Reserve the liquid.

2 Scrub the potatoes clean with a brush under the tap and cook in salted water. Cut into four, leaving the skin on.

3 Strain the liquid in which the ceps soaked through a fine sieve. Peel the garlic and crush. Bring the strained liquid to the boil together the cream and garlic, add the ceps and simmer for about 5 minutes. Add the thickening agent and season with salt and pepper.

4 Wipe the field mushrooms with kitchen paper, prepare and cut into thick slices. Fry them in hot oil. Add to the potatoes together with the parsley and stir. Season with salt and pepper.

5 Arrange the potato and mushroom mixture in a greased gratin dish and pour the cep and cream sauce over all. Cut the cheese into small cubes and sprinkle on top. Preheat the oven to 200°C (400°F), Gas mark 6 and bake on the middle shelf for about 30 minutes.

Serves 4. About 600 kcal per serving.

20 g/¾ oz dried ceps (wild mushrooms)

1 kg/2¼ lb small potatoes

salt

250 ml/8 fl oz (1 cup) cream

1 clove garlic

2 tablespoons sauce thickening agent

freshly ground pepper from the mill

500 g/18 oz field mushrooms

4 tablespoons oil

2 tablespoons dried parsley

200 g/7 oz fontina or Gruyère cheese

Baked
cheese dishes

Cheese soufflé

A cheese soufflé is a light, airy dish that many cooks would love to make but are frightened to attempt. But the only essential condition is not to open the oven during the baking process. If curiosity is controlled, nothing can go wrong. Depending on taste, Emmental, Gouda or a more powerful cheese such as Appenzell may be used. Chopped herbs can also be added to the mixture, making a soufflé that can be served with a salad as a light main meal.

1 Melt the butter in a pan over medium heat, add the flour and sweat until golden. Gradually add the milk while stirring. Continue stirring briskly to prevent lumps from forming until the mixture is smooth and thick. Remove from the heat and leave to cool a little.

2 Separate the eggs and add the egg yolks one by one to the mixture, folding them in carefully. Add the cheese and season generously with lemon juice, salt, pepper and nutmeg.

3 Grease a round glass soufflé dish (about 24 cm/9½ in) with soft butter and sprinkle with breadcrumbs.

4 Beat the egg whites until stiff and fold gently into the mixture. Carefully spoon this mixture into the soufflé dish and bake on the second shelf of the oven preheated to 200°C (400°F), Gas mark 6 for 30 minutes until golden brown. Do not open the oven during this time. Serve immediately.

Serves 4. About 525 kcal per serving.

60 g/2 oz (4 tablespoons) butter

60 g/2 oz (½ cup) flour

250 ml/8 fl oz (1 cup) milk

5 eggs

200 g/7 oz (1¾ cups) grated
   hard cheese

1 tablespoon lemon juice

salt

freshly ground pepper
   from the mill

freshly ground nutmeg

butter for the dish

3 tablespoons breadcrumbs

Quince and pear gratin with cheese

The sharp flavours of the quince and pears go very well with cheese. Depending on taste you a milder or sharper cheese may be used, such as unpasteurised Brie, Munster or one of the blue cheeses. Served with crispy white bread and a glass of wine, this gratin makes a delicious snack to enjoy with friends.

❶ Peel the quince, cut into quarters, remove the core and slice into thin strips. Sprinkle with lemon juice to prevent them going brown. Peel the shallots and chop finely.

❷ Heat 2 tablespoons oil in a saucepan, add the shallots and fry until transparent. Add the quince and the wine. Cover and simmer gently for about 20 minutes. Wash the thyme, remove the leaves from the stem, chop finely and add to the quince. Season with salt and pepper.

❸ Wash the pears, cut into quarters, remove the core and cut into thin strips.

❹ Remove the quince from the pan and reduce the juice by half over high heat.

❺ Arrange the quince and pears in alternate layers in a soufflé dish and pour the reduced juice on top. Sprinkle with pumpkin seeds and season with pepper.

❻ Bake for about 10 minutes on the middle shelf in the oven preheated to 200°C (400°F), Gas mark 6. Cut the cheese into slices and place on top, sprinkle with the rest of the oil and bake on the top shelf of the oven until the cheese has melted. But do not let it turn golden or brown.

Serves 4. About 450 kcal per serving.

2 quinces

juice of 1 lemon

2 shallots

4 tablespoons walnut oil

100 ml/3½ fl oz (½ cup) dry
    white wine

2 sprigs thyme

salt

freshly ground pepper
    from the mill

2 Williams pears

2 tablespoons pumpkin seeds

200 g/7 oz ripe Camembert

Pasta gratin with mixed cheeses

When making this dish it is important to cook the pasta for only a very short time so that it can absorb the liquid in the sauce without becoming too soft. It is delicious served with a tomato sauce.

400 g/14 oz macaroni

salt

60 g/2 oz (4 tablespoons) butter

50 g/2 oz (½ cup) flour

500 ml/17 fl oz (2¼ cups) milk

freshly ground pepper from the mill

freshly ground nutmeg

50 g/2 oz (½ cup) chopped Gorgonzola

50 g/2 oz (½ cup) grated Gouda

50 g/2 oz (½ cup) grated Parmesan

50 g/2 oz (½ cup) grated Appenzell or Gruyère

1 Cook the macaroni briefly in plenty of boiling salted water, drain and stir in 15 g/½ oz (1 tablespoon) butter.

2 Melt the butter in a saucepan and continue heating until it becomes frothy. Add the flour, fry until golden and stir in the milk slowly while stirring. Simmer for 5 minutes, stirring constantly. Stir half the four cheeses into the bechamel sauce and allow to melt. Season generously with salt, pepper and nutmeg.

3 Stir the cheese sauce into the pasta and spoon into a gratin dish. Sprinkle the rest of the cheese on top and bake on the middle shelf of the oven, preheated to 200°C (400°F), Gas mark 6, for about 30 minutes until ready.

Serves 4. About 790 kcal per serving.

Chicken breasts in Gorgonzola sauce

This creamy Gorgonzola sauce is a delicious way of serving tender chicken breasts. The same method can be used with other vegetables such as carrots or broccoli. The dish is delicious served with green tagliatelle or simply with crisp white bread.

❶ Cook the peas and spinach in a little salted water in separate saucepans until just tender, then drain. Wipe the mushrooms with kitchen paper, clean and cut into half or quarters depending on their size.

❷ Rinse the chicken fillets and pat dry. Heat 3 tablespoons oil in a saucepan. Wash the sage leaves, pat dry and fry the chicken briefly on both sides for about 3 minutes in the same oil over a high heat. Remove from the heat.

❸ Now add the mushrooms to the pan and fry until golden brown, stirring constantly. Season with salt and pepper.

❹ Heat the cream in a small saucepan, add the finely diced Gorgonzola and let it melt in the cream. Season with salt and pepper and a dash of lemon juice.

❺ Grease a shallow soufflé dish with the rest of the oil. Arrange the spinach, peas and mushrooms in it. Cut the chicken breasts into slices and place them on top.

❻ Pour the cheese and cream mixture over all and bake on the second shelf from the top of the oven, preheated to 180°C (350°F), Gas mark 4, for 15–20 minutes until golden brown.

Serves 4. About 530 kcal per serving.

300 g/10 oz frozen peas

300 g/10 oz frozen spinach

salt

500 g/18 oz mushrooms

4 chicken breasts, without skin

4 tablespoons olive oil

10 leaves fresh sage

freshly ground white pepper from the mill

200 ml/7 fl oz (⅞ cup) cream

150 g/5 oz Gorgonzola

a dash of lemon juice

Spinach nests with goat's cheese

Inspired by Mediterranean cuisine, this dish has a delicious fragrance, reminiscent of summer holidays. Served in little ramekins, it is very decorative and makes an original starter when guests are invited. Use a mild goat's cheese for this dish.

300 g/10 oz frozen spinach

salt

1 onion

4 tablespoons olive oil

2 tablespoons dried tomatoes in oil and 4 tablespoons of the oil

4 pickled artichoke hearts

freshly ground pepper from the mill

1 tablespoon herbes de Provence

¼ piece pitta bread

2 tablespoons pine kernels

200 g/7 oz goat's cheese

❶ Thaw the spinach in a little salted water and drain. Peel the onions and chop finely.

❷ Fry the chopped onions briefly in 2 tablespoons until golden. Drain the dried tomatoes and artichoke hearts and cut into fine strips. Add both to the pan and fry briefly. Season with salt, pepper and the herbes de Provence.

❸ Cut the pitta bread into small cubes and stir into the tomato and artichoke mixture. Add the pine kernels and tomato oil.

❹ Grease four small ramekins with oil and arrange the spinach in them. Put the tomato mixture on top. Cut the goat's cheese into thin slices and cover the spinach nests with it. Sprinkle the remaining oil on top and bake in the oven, preheated to 200°C (400°F), Gas mark 6, on the second shelf from the top for about 15-20 minutes.

Serves 4. About 490 kcal per serving.

Polenta with Gorgonzola

Polenta is a very popular in Northern Italy and can be prepared in many ways. Take care that it does not burn while cooking because it may stick at the beginning. Instant ("one-minute") polenta can be used if time is short, but it is less satisfactory.

salt

300 g/10 oz polenta flour

4 beef tomatoes

2 sweet red peppers

4 tablespoons oil

200 g/7 oz Gorgonzola

freshly ground pepper
   from the mill

❶ Bring 1.5 litres/2¾ pints (7 cups) water to the boil with a little salt and slowly add the polenta, stirring all the time. Continue stirring and cook the polenta for about 40 minutes over a low heat until soft. Rinse a chopping board under cold water and roll out the polenta on it to a thickness of 2 cm/¾ in. Leave to cool.

❷ Make a cross in the tomatoes and blanch in boiling water. Remove from the water and peel. Cut the tomatoes into quarters, remove the stalks and seeds and cut into large cubes.

❸ Wash the peppers, cut in half and remove the seeds. Press flat on a baking sheet and cook under the grill until the skin turns brown. Cover with a damp cloth and leave to cool. Peel the peppers and cut into thin strips.

❹ Cut the polenta into pieces about 10 x 10 cm/4 x 4 in square. Heat the oil in a pan and fry the polenta until golden brown.

❺ Remove the rind of the Gorgonzola and cut into small cubes. Arrange the polenta portions diagonally in a gratin dish, alternating with peppers and tomatoes. Season with salt and pepper.

❻ Sprinkle with the cubed Gorgonzola and bake for about 25 minutes on the second shelf from the top in the oven preheated to 200°C (400°F), Gas mark 6.

Serves 4. About 580 kcal per serving.

Panzerotti with white cabbage and Gorgonzola

Panzerotti are little pasta parcels with a filling, available frozen in shops and supermarkets. Choose the filling according to taste, either vegetarian or with ham.

❶ Wash the white cabbage, cut into quarters and remove the stalk. Cut each quarter into thin strips and blanch in boiling salted water for about 3 minutes. Run briefly under cold water and drain.

❷ Cook the panzerotti in plenty of boiling salted water until "al dente". Drain. Stir the strips of white cabbage into the panzerotti and place in a soufflé dish.

❸ Heat the crème fraîche in a small saucepan. Cut the Gorgonzola into small cubes, add to the cream and stir until melted. Add the wine, bring to the boil and simmer briefly. Season with salt and pepper.

❹ Pour the cheese sauce over the pasta and white cabbage and sprinkle with Parmesan. Bake on the middle shelf in the oven, preheated to 200°C (400°F), Gas mark 6. for about 20 minutes.

Serves 4. About 1030 kcal per serving.

1 small white cabbage, about 500 g/18 oz

salt

500 g/18 oz panzerotti

300 g/10 oz crème fraîche

150 g/5 oz Gorgonzola

50 ml/1½ fl oz (3 tablespoons) white wine

freshly ground pepper from the mill

75 g/3 oz (¾ cup) grated Parmesan

Broccoli gratin with cheese

1 kg/2¼ lb broccoli

salt

60 g/2 oz (4 tablespoons) butter

60 g/2 oz (½ cup) flour

320ml/11 fl oz (1⅜ cups) milk

2 eggs

250 ml/8 fl oz (1 cup) cream

150 g/6 oz (1½ cups) freshly
   grated Gouda

freshly ground white pepper
   from the mill

freshly ground nutmeg

4 tablespoons chopped hazelnuts

This gratin takes some time to make but it tastes absolutely delicious and is also relatively inexpensive.

1 Wash the broccoli, separate the florets and remove the stalks. Peel the stalks and cut into pieces 2 cm/¾ in long. Blanch the broccoli florets and stalks in 2 litres/3½ pints (9 cups) boiling salted water. Plunge into cold water and drain.

2 Melt the butter in a saucepan, stir in the flour and cook until smooth. Add the milk and cream, stirring constantly. Simmer gently over a low heat for about 20 minutes, stirring occasionally. Remove the sauce from the heat. Separate the eggs. Add a little sauce to the egg yolks, stir in 50 g/2 oz (½ cup) cheese and return to the rest of the sauce. Season with salt, pepper and nutmeg. Add a pinch of salt, beat the egg-whites until stiff and fold carefully into the sauce.

3 Grease a tall-sided soufflé dish with some butter and sprinkle 1 tablespoon chopped hazelnuts into it. Pour half the sauce into the gratin dish, arrange the broccoli on top and cover with the rest of the sauce. Sprinkle the rest of the hazelnuts and cheese on top.

4 Preheat the oven to 180°C (350°F), Gas mark 4 and bake on the middle shelf for about 1 hour.

Serves 4. About 590 kcal per serving.

Penne and ewes' milk cheese

This gratin has a pleasant sharpish taste because of the ewes' milk cheese.

1 Cook the penne in plenty of boiling salted water and drain.

2 Cut the ewes' milk cheese into small cubes. Wash and prepare the courgettes and pepper. Cut the courgette into sticks about 3 cm/1¼ in long and the pepper into 2 cm/¾ in cubes. Peel the onions and cut into thin rings. Wipe the mushrooms clean with kitchen paper, trim and cut into quarters. Sprinkle with lemon juice.

3 Stir the cheese cubes and vegetables into the penne. Season with salt and pepper.

4 Separate the eggs. Whisk the egg yolks into the cream and Parmesan and stir into the vegetable and penne mixture. Beat the egg whites until stiff and fold carefully into the penne and vegetables.

5 Place the penne mixture in a greased gratin dish. Preheat the oven to 200°C (400°F), Gas mark 6 and bake on the middle shelf for about 45 minutes.

Serves 4. About 560 kcal per serving.

150 g/5 oz penne

salt

200 g/7 oz ewes' milk cheese

1 small courgette (zucchini)

1 sweet pepper (red or yellow)

2 onions

100 g/3½ oz mushrooms

1 tablespoon lemon juice

freshly ground pepper
   from the mill

4 eggs

250 ml/8 fl oz (1 cup) cream

75 g/3 oz (¾ cup) grated
   Parmesan

Cheese spätzle

Spätzle are little dumplings, a speciality of Alsace and southern Germany. This Swabian speciality is delicious served with a green salad.

❶ Put the flour in a bowl. Add the eggs, a pinch of salt and sufficient water to make a heavy dough. Beat this batter until it forms bubbles.

❷ Grease a gratin dish with oil and put to one side. Heat 2 litres/3½ pints (9 cups) salted water in a large saucepan. Drop the spätzle dough spoonful by spoonful into the boiling water and with the aid of another spoon form them into dumplings. When the spätzle rise to the surface, remove them, drain and place in the gratin dish. Sprinkle a little cheese on top and season with pepper. Repeat this process until all the dough has been used.

❸ Preheat the oven to 200°C (400°F), Gas mark 6 and bake the cheese spätzle on the middle shelf for about15 minutes.

❹ Peel the onions and cut into thin rings. Heat a little oil in a pan, add the onions and fry until golden brown. Pour over the cheese spätzle.

Serves 4. About 860 kcal per serving.

500 g/18 oz (5 cups) flour

6 eggs

salt

4 tablespoons oil

300 g/10 oz (2½ cups) freshly grated cheese (Gouda or Emmental)

freshly ground pepper from the mill

4 onions

Baked
desserts

Semolina gratin

This semolina gratin is a delicious pudding enjoyed by both adults and children. It can be served hot or cold with a variety of sauces or fruit compotes.

500 ml/17 fl oz (2¼ cups) milk

50 g/2 oz (¼ cup) sugar

1 packet vanilla sugar

1 pinch salt

zest of 1 untreated
  lemon

80 g/3 oz (2 cups) semolina

2 eggs

50 g/2 oz (4 tablespoons) butter

50 g/2 oz (⅜ cup) flaked (slivered)
  almonds

icing (confectioners') sugar

1 Add the sugar, vanilla sugar, salt and lemon zest to the milk and bring to the boil. Next add the semolina, stirring constantly. Simmer gently over low heat for about 10 minutes.

2 Separate the eggs. Carefully stir 2 tablespoons of the semolina mixture into make sure that the egg yolks do not curdle. Then add to the rest of the semolina.

3 Beat the egg whites into stiff peaks and carefully fold into the semolina with a spatula.

4 Butter a gratin dish and carefully spoon the semolina mixture into it. Level off and dot the rest of the butter on top. Sprinkle with flaked (slivered) almonds. Preheat the oven to 200°C (400°F), Gas mark 6 and bake on the middle shelf for about 20 minutes. Sprinkle with icing (confectioners') sugar just before serving.

Serves 4. About 435 kcal per serving.

Semolina gratin with apple and pear compote

In this recipe, the semolina is baked in small ramekins and served with a tasty fruit compote. The dish can be served lukewarm or cold and will add a festive note to any meal.

1 Melt the butter and coat four ramekins with it, then sprinkle with sugar.

2 Cut the vanilla pod lengthways and remove the flesh. Add both the vanilla pod and flesh to the milk in a pan together with 50 g/2 oz (¼ cup) sugar and bring to the boil. Add the semolina and salt little by little, stirring constantly, and simmer over low heat for about 15 minutes. Pour into a bowl and leave to cool, stirring occasionally.

3 For the compote, peel the apples and pears, cut into quarters, remove the core, cut into thin slices and sprinkle with lemon juice.

4 Caramelise 70 g/3 oz (⅜ cup) sugar in a thick-bottomed pan and stir in the wine and lemon juice. Cook until the caramel has dissolved completely in the wine and juice. Add the apple and pear slices to the caramel juice. Simmer over a low heat but do not overcook. Take the fruit out of the pan and reduce the juice by half over high heat. Pour over the fruit and leave to cool.

5 Separate the eggs, beat the egg yolks and add to the semolina together with the lemon zest. Beat the egg whites very stiff while gradually adding the rest of the sugar. Fold the beaten egg whites carefully into the semolina mixture and pour into the four ramekins.

6 Place the ramekins in a roasting tin filled with two fingers of boiling water. Preheat the oven to 180°C (350°F), Gas mark 4 and bake on the middle shelf for about 20 minutes.

7 When lukewarm or cold, loosen the semolina all round with a knife and turn out onto a dish. Decorate with fruit slices all round and pour the juice over all.

Serves 4. About 664 kcal per serving.

---

1 tablespoon butter

175 g/6 oz (¾ cup) sugar

1 vanilla pod

750 ml/1¼ pints (3½ cups) milk

100 g/3½ oz (⅔ cup) semolina

1 pinch salt

6 eggs

zest and juice of 1 untreated lemon

2 Williams pears

2 Bramley or other tart apples

200 ml/7 fl oz (⅞ cup) white wine

200 ml/7 fl oz (⅞ cup) apple juice

Semolina gratin with cherries

500 g/18 oz cherries

½ vanilla pod

500 ml/17 fl oz (2¼ cups) milk

100 g/3½ oz (⅔ cup) semolina

100 g/4 oz (½ cup) soft butter

4 eggs

100 g/4 oz (½ cup) sugar

grated zest of 1 untreated lemon

This gratin will be popular with both adults and children. For a change sour cherries may be used, and if time is short, canned cherries will work well. This gratin is also delicious cold.

❶ Wash the cherries and stone them.

❷ Bring the milk to the boil with the vanilla pod in it. Add the semolina gradually, stirring constantly, and simmer over low heat for about 10–15 minutes.

❸ Butter a gratin dish.

❹ Separate the eggs and beat the egg yolks with the sugar and 75g/3 oz (6 tablespoons) butter until foamy. Add the semolina mixture together with the lemon zest.

❺ Beat the egg whites until they form stiff peaks and carefully fold into the semolina mixture. Spoon half the semolina into the gratin dish, arrange the cherries on top and cover with the rest of the semolina.

❻ Dot the rest of the butter on top. Preheat the oven to 200°C (400°F), Gas mark 6 and bake on the middle shelf for about 30 minutes.

Serves 4. About 620 kcal per serving.

Ricotta and cherry gratin with almond topping

This gratin is particularly delicious with sour cherries. It can also be made with apricots or damson plums – always sour fruit.

1 Wash the cherries, stone them, sprinkle with 100 g/3½ oz (½ cup) and cinnamon and leave to stand for 1 hour for the juice to come out. Pour the juice into a pan and heat. Add a little water to the thickening agent and stir until you obtain a smooth mixture. Then add to the boiling juice. Continue stirring until the juice has thickened, add the cherries and simmer gently for about 5 minutes. Remove from the heat and leave to cool.

2 To make the almond topping, cream together 100 g/4 oz (½ cup) butter with 100 g/3½ oz (½ cup) sugar and stir in half the lemon zest and the ground almonds.

3 To make the ricotta mixture, melt 50 g/2 oz (4 tablespoons) butter. Beat the egg yolk with 50 g/2 oz (¼ cup) sugar and the vanilla sugar until foamy, then add the ricotta, semolina, the melted butter and the rest of the lemon zest. Beat the egg whites until they form stiff peaks, adding 25 g/1 oz (2 tablespoons) sugar little by little.

4 Butter a gratin dish with the rest of the butter and sprinkle with breadcrumbs. Fill with half the ricotta mixture, spread a layer of cherry compote on top and cover with the rest of the ricotta mixture. Finally, pour the almond topping over it.

5 Sprinkle with almond flakes, preheat the oven to 180°C (350°F), Gas mark 4 and bake on the middle shelf for about 40 minutes. Sprinkle with icing (confectioners') sugar before serving.

Serves 4. About 1060 kcal per serving.

500 g/18 oz sour cherries

280 g/10 oz (1⅓ cups) sugar

½ teaspoon cinnamon

30 g/1 oz thickening agent

160 g/6 oz (¾ cup) soft butter

grated zest of 1 untreated lemon

100 g/3½ oz (¾ cup) ground almonds

3 egg whites

1 packet vanilla sugar

500 g/18 oz ricotta

75 g/3 oz (¾ cup) semolina flour

2 tablespoons breadcrumbs

30 g/1 oz (⅓ cup) flaked (slivered) almond

icing (confectioners') sugar

500 g/18 oz red currants

100 g/3½ oz (½ cup) sugar

2 tablespoons rum

120 g/4 oz (1 cup) hazelnuts

3 eggs

30 g/1 oz (¼ cup) flour

30 g/1 oz thickening agent

1 level teaspoons baking powder

zest of 1 untreated lemon

75 g/3 oz (½ cup) flaked (slivered)
   hazelnuts

½ teaspoon cinnamon

2 tablespoons brown sugar

Red currant and nut gratin

The tart taste of the red currants contrasts pleasantly with the sweet nutty topping. Serve this gratin as a pudding after a light meal or as a sweet main meal. Other sour berries or fruits can be used to make this gratin and other kinds of nuts can be used for the topping.

1 Wash the red currants and strip them from the stalks. Put in a greased gratin dish and stir in 1 tablespoon each of sugar and rum.

2 Preheat the oven to 200°C (400°F), Gas mark 6. Spread the hazelnuts on a baking sheet and roast for about 15 minutes. Rub the brown skin off the hazelnuts with a cloth and grind the hazelnuts finely in a mill or pestle and mortar.

3 Whisk half the remaining sugar into the egg yolks and beat until the mixture becomes pale. Beat the egg whites until stiff and carefully fold in the rest of the sugar. Mix together the flour, thickening agent, baking powder and ground hazelnuts and pour onto the beaten egg white mixture. Then fold gently into the egg yolk cream.

4 Pour this egg mixture on top of the red currants. Mix together the flaked (slivered) hazelnuts, cinnamon and brown sugar.

5 Preheat the oven to 200°C (400°F), Gas mark 6 and bake on the middle shelf for about 25 minutes.

Serves 4. About 640 kcal per serving.

Ricotta gratin with apricots

This tasty dish can be refrigerated after cooking and eaten cold. It is also delicious with other fruit such as peaches or damsons.

❶ Wash the apricots, cut in half and remove the stones. Soak the raisins in rum.

❷ Butter a gratin dish or ring mould. Separate the eggs and beat the egg yolks with 50 g/2 oz (¼ cup) sugar and the rest of the butter until foamy. Stir in the ricotta, blancmange powder, lemon-juice and lemon zest.

❸ Beat the egg whites until stiff and gently fold in the rest of the sugar. Next carefully fold the beaten egg whites into the ricotta mixture. Then spoon it into the gratin dish and level off.

❹ Press the apricot halves into the ricotta mixture with the cut surface downwards. Preheat the oven and bake on the second shelf from the bottom for about 45 minutes. Sprinkle with icing (confectioners') sugar just before serving.

Serves 4. About 470 kcal per serving.

500 g/18 oz apricots

2 tablespoons raisins

2 tablespoons rum

60 g/2 oz (4 tablespoons) soft butter

3 eggs

100 g/3½ oz (½ cup) sugar

500 g/18 oz ricotta

1 packet blancmange powder (for 500 ml/17 fl oz (2¼ cups) milk)

juice and zest of 1 untreated lemon

icing (confectioners') sugar

Ricotta macaroni gratin

This gratin is quick and easy to make and is particularly popular with children. Serve hot or cold with fruit compote or vanilla sauce. It can be made with left-over pasta.

❶ Add a pinch of salt to the milk and bring to the boil. Add the pasta and cook over low heat but do not overcook. Leave to cool.

❷ Separate the eggs and whisk the egg yolks with the sugar until foamy. Next add the ricotta and crème fraîche and stir in the pasta.

❸ Beat the egg whites very stiff and fold carefully into the pasta mixture with a spatula. Pour into a buttered gratin dish, preheat the oven to 200°C (400°F), Gas mark 6 and bake on the middle shelf for about 30 minutes.

Serves 4. About 570 kcal per serving.

500 ml/17 fl oz (2¼ cups) milk

1 pinch salt

200 g/7 oz short pasta

3 eggs

75g/2½ oz (⅓ cup) sugar

250 g/9 oz ricotta

100 ml/3½ fl oz (½ cup) crème fraîche

butter for the dish

Strawberry and egg bake

❶ Wash, clean and hull the strawberries, then cut them in half. Sprinkle with 50 g/2 oz (¼ cup) sugar and leave for about an hour.

❷ Separate the eggs. Whisk the yolk to a creamy mass with 50 g/2 oz (¼ cup) sugar. Beat the egg whites with the remaining sugar into stiff peaks. Combine the strawberries with the yolk mixture, lemon juice, cinnamon and hazelnuts. Carefully fold in the whisked egg whites.

❸ Fill a buttered casserole dish with the mixture and cook on the middle shelf of a pre-heated oven for 30–40 minutes. Dust before serving with icing (confectioners') sugar.

Serves 4. About 465 kcal per serving.

750 g/1½ lb strawberries

150 g/5 oz (⅔ cup) sugar

3 eggs

juice of ½ lemon

1 tablespoon cinnamon

100 g/3½ oz (¾ cup) ground hazelnuts

butter for the dish

icing (confectioners') sugar

Blackberry and ricotta gratin

The ricotta topping conceals a mouth-watering fruit compote that also acts as a sauce. Any fruit can be used to make this gratin which looks very pretty in a heat-resistant glass gratin dish. It is delicious served hot with vanilla ice cream.

500 g/18 oz blackberries

60 g/2 oz (4 tablespoons) soft butter

2 eggs

100 g/3½ oz (½ cup) sugar

1 vanilla pod

500 g/18 oz ricotta

zest and juice of 1 untreated lemon

75 g/3 oz (¾ cup) flour

1 level teaspoons baking powder

100 g/3½ oz (1 cup) shelled walnuts

3 tablespoons brown sugar

❶ Wash the blackberries and drain well. Butter a gratin dish and arrange the blackberries in it.

❷ Separate the eggs, beat the egg yolks with 50 g/2 oz (¼ cup) sugar until foamy. Cut the vanilla pod lengthways, remove the pulp and stir into the egg mixture together with the ricotta. Wash the lemon in hot water, wipe dry, grate the zest thinly and squeeze the juice. Add the juice and zest to the ricotta mixture.

❸ Beat the egg whites very stiffly with the rest of the sugar and carefully add to the ricotta mixture. Sieve the baking powder and flour over the egg and ricotta mixture and fold in carefully using a spatula.

❹ Cover the blackberries with this mixture. Chop the walnuts coarsely, mix with the brown sugar and sprinkle over the gratin. Preheat the oven to 200°C (400°F), Gas mark 6 and bake on the second shelf from the bottom for about 40 minutes.

Serves 6. About 455 kcal per serving.

500 g/18 oz rhubarb

2 eggs

500 g/18 oz ricotta

1 vanilla pod

250 g/9 oz (generous 1 cup) sugar

zest and juice of 1 untreated
  lemon

60 g/2 oz (½ cup) semolina flour

½ packet baking powder

butter for the dish

Rhubarb and ricotta gratin

This ricotta and semolina mixture is ideal for baking with many different
kinds of fruit. Instead of rhubarb, stone fruit or berries may be used.
Serve with a fruit or vanilla sauce. The gratin is also delicious cold,
when it can be cut into slices.

❶ Wash the rhubarb, peel and cut into pieces 3 cm/1¼ in long .

❷ Separate the eggs. Mix together the ricotta and the pulp of the vanilla pod
with the egg yolks and sugar. Wash the lemon in hot water and dry carefully.
Then grate thinly and squeeze the juice. Stir the zest and juice into the ricotta
mixture.

❸ Stir the baking powder into the semolina and fold in the ricotta mixture.
Next add the rhubarb pieces.

❹ Beat the egg whites until stiff and carefully fold into the semolina and ricotta
mixture with a spatula.

❺ Butter a gratin dish, spoon the mixture into it and level off. Preheat the oven
to 180°C (350°F), Gas mark 4 and bake on the middle shelf for about 1 hour.

Serves 4. About 530 kcal per serving.

Pears on a bed of ricotta

This dish is particularly attractive when served in individual ramekins. Use ripe pears because they have much more flavour. For special occasions, serve with a raspberry or blackberry coulis.

1 Peel the pears but do not remove the stalks. Roll immediately in lemon juice to prevent them from going brown.

2 Coat four ramekins with melted butter and sprinkle with breadcrumbs. Place the pears upright in the ramkins.

3 Separate the eggs and beat the egg yolk with the sugar and softened butter until very foamy. Add the baking powder to the semolina and stir into the egg mixture. Wash the lemon in hot water, wipe dry, grate the zest thinly and squeeze the juice. Add the juice and zest together with the ricotta to the egg mixture.

4 Beat the egg whites into stiff peaks and carefully fold in the egg yolk mixture with a spatula. Arrange around the pears with a spoon. Pour the rest of the melted butter over the pears and sprinkle with flaked (slivered) almonds.

5 Preheat the oven to 180°C (350°F), Gas mark 4 and bake on the middle shelf for about 35 minutes.

Serves 4. About 680 kcal per serving.

4 Williams pears

squeeze lemon juice

50 g/2 oz (4 tablespoons) melted butter

2 tablespoons breadcrumbs

4 eggs

100 g/3½ oz (½ cup) sugar

80 g/3 oz (6 tablespoons) soft butter

50 g/2 oz (⅓ cup) semolina flour

½ packet baking powder

zest and juice of 1 untreated lemon

500 g/18 oz ricotta

2 tablespoons flaked (slivered) almond

Delicate ricotta gratin with bananas

The light ricotta topping conceals pieces of nougat and bananas. It looks particularly attractive when served cold and cut into slices, garnished with rum-flavoured cream.

4 eggs

120 g/4 oz (generous ½ cup) sugar

75 g/3 oz (½ cup) semolina

2 level teaspoons baking powder

500 g/18 oz ricotta

zest of 1 untreated lemon

4 bananas

100 g/3½ oz block of nougat

30 g/1 oz (2 tablespoons) butter

4 tablespoons ground hazelnuts

❶ Separate the eggs. Beat the egg yolks with the sugar until foamy. Add the baking powder to the semolina and stir it into the egg yolk mixture together with the ricotta and the lemon zest.

❷ Beat the egg-whites very stiff and fold carefully into the mixture.

❸ Peel the bananas and cut the nougat into strips.

❹ Butter an oblong gratin dish. Spoon half the ricotta mixture into it and level off. Arrange the bananas and lengths of nougat alternately on top. Sprinkle with ground hazelnuts and cover with the rest of the ricotta mixture.

❺ Dot the rest of the butter in flakes over the dish, preheat the oven to 200°C (400°F), Gas mark 6 and bake on the middle shelf for about 35 minutes.

Serves 4. About 700 kcal per serving.

Spoon bread

This sweet baked soufflé bread comes from South Carolina. It tastes best when the inside is still slightly moist.

300 ml/10 fl oz (1¼ cups) cream

300 ml/10 fl oz (1¼ cups) milk

60 g/2 oz (4 tablespoons) butter

60 g/2 oz (4 tablespoons) honey

1/2 teaspoon salt

150 g/5 oz (1 cup) maize flour
(corn meal)

6 egg yolks

1 teaspoon baking powder

4 egg whites

50 g/2 oz (¼ cup) sugar

icing (confectioners') sugar

❶ Put the cream, milk, butter, honey and salt in a pan and warm over a low heat, stirring constantly until the butter has melted. Slowly add the maize flour (corn meal) and stir constantly for 20 minutes until it has swelled.

❷ Put the batter in a bowl and stir in the egg yolks one by one. Mix in the baking powder. Beat the egg whites with the sugar until stiff. Fold the egg whites into the mixture.

❸ Spoon the mixture into a buttered soufflé dish. Cook for 35 minutes in the oven preheated to 190°C (375°F), Gas mark 5. Remove the spoon bread from the oven and sprinkle with icing (confectioners') sugar. Serve from the dish with a spoon.

Serves 4. About 485 kcal per serving.

Millet gratin with apples

Millet is very digestible and delicious in sweet dishes. The raisins can be soaked in rum if the dish is not for children.

❶ Rinse the millet in a sieve. Mix the cream with the apple juice , bring to the boil and add the millet. Simmer over a very low heat for about 20 minutes.

❷ Wash the lemon thoroughly, wipe dry, grate the zest and squeeze the juice. Peel the apples, cut into quarters, remove the core and cut into thin slices. Stir in the lemon juice together with 40 g/11/2 oz (1½ tablespoons) sugar.

❸ Separate the eggs, beat the egg yolks with the rest of the sugar until very foamy and stir in the lemon zest. Beat the egg whites until they form stiff peaks.

❹ Butter a gratin dish. Mix the apples and raisins together.

❺ Stir the egg yolk mixture into the millet and carefully fold in the beaten egg whites. Pour half this mixture into the gratin dish, arrange the apples on top and cover with the rest of the mixture.

❻ Dot the rest of the butter in flakes over the gratin, preheat the oven to 200°C (400°F), Gas mark 6 and bake on the middle shelf for 50 – 60 minutes. Sprinkle with icing (confectioners') sugar just before serving.

Serves 4. About 715 kcal per serving.

250 g/9 oz (2½ cups) millet

250 ml/8 fl oz (1 cup) cream

500 ml/17 fl oz (2¼ cups) apple juice

zest and juice of 1 untreated lemon

4 Bramley or other tart apples

80 g/3 oz (⅜ cup) sugar

2 eggs

30 g/1 oz (2 tablespoons) butter

50 g/2 oz (⅓ cup) raisins

icing (confectioners') sugar

Tipsy strawberries

600 g/1¼ lb strawberries

30 g/1 oz (2 tablespoons) butter

20 g/¾ oz (1½ tablespoons) sugar

1 packet vanilla sugar

4 tablespoons brandy

125 ml/4 fl oz (½ cup) cream

4 egg yolks

icing (confectioners') sugar

❶ Wash, clean and hull the strawberries, then cut in half. Spread the strawberries evenly in four small ovenproof dishes or large ramekins.

❷ Melt the butter in the double boiler melts. Little by little stir in the sugar, vanilla sugar, brandy, cream and egg yolk, and beat to a stiff cream.

❸ Spread the mixture over the strawberries. Preheat the oven to 200°C (400°F), Gas mark 6 and cook on the middle shelf for 40 minutes.. Remove from the oven, leave to cool a little and sprinkle with icing (confectioners') sugar. Serve the dish warm.

Serves 4. About 285 kcal per serving.

Apple and nut gratin

75 g/3 oz (½ cup) flaked (slivered) almonds

4 Bramley or other tart apples

juice of 1 lemon

75 g/3 oz marzipan

5 eggs

2 tablespoons rum

70 g/3 oz (⅓ cup) sugar

1 tablespoon cinnamon

375 g/13 oz (3¾ cups) flour

500 ml/17 fl oz (2¼ cups) milk

butter for the dish

The apples are filled with a marzipan mixture and baked in an egg pastry. The dish should not be too deep because the pastry should envelop the apples as high as possible.

❶ Fry the almond flakes in a non-stick pan without fat until golden yellow.

❷ Peel the apples and remove the core with an apple corer. Halve the apples lengthways. Roll them immediately in lemon juice to prevent them from going brown.

❸ Beat the sugar with 4 egg yolks until foamy and stir in the cinnamon, flour and milk. Beat the egg whites until stiff and carefully fold in the egg yolk mixture with a spatula.

❹ Butter a gratin dish and line the bottom with the apple halves with their cut surface upward. Spread the marzipan paste over the apples and pour the batter over all. Preheat the oven to 200°C (400°F), Gas mark 6 and bake on the middle shelf for about 50 minutes.

Serves 4. About 885 kcal per serving.

Apple gratin with kumquats

Kumquats are small citrus fruits can that can be eaten with the skin on. If kumquats are not available, the zest from untreated oranges and candied orange peel can be used. It is a perfect adult pudding for a special occasion and should be served with vanilla ice cream and whipped cream.

❶ Sprinkle rum over the sultanas and leave to soak for at least 1 hour.

❷ Peel the apples, cut into quarters, remove the core and cut into slices. Wash the lemon in hot water, wipe dry, grate thinly and squeeze the juice out. Add the juice and zest to the sliced apples.

❸ Wash the kumquats and cut diagonally into thin slices. Add the kumquats and sultanas to the sliced apples and put the fruit mixture in a gratin dish. Sprinkle with 2 tablespoons of sugar. Preheat the oven to 200°C (400°F), Gas mark 6 and bake on the middle shelf for about 15 minutes.

❹ Separate the eggs and beat the egg yolks with 50 g/2 oz (¼ cup) sugar until foamy. Beat the egg whites into stiff peaks with the rest of the sugar and add to the egg yolk mixture. Sieve the flour over it and fold in with a spatula.

❺ Remove the gratin from the oven and cover the fruit with the egg mixture. Sprinkle with almond flakes. Return to the oven and bake for another 15 minutes until ready. The top should be golden brown. Sprinkle with icing (confectioners') sugar just before serving.

Serves 4. About 415 kcal per serving.

2 tablespoons sultanas

2 tablespoons Rum

3 Bramley or other tart apples

zest and juice of 1 untreated lemon

12 kumquats

3 eggs

120 g/4 oz (½ cup) sugar

40 g/1½ oz (½ cup) flour

40 g/1½ oz (½ cup) flaked (slivered) almonds

butter for the dish

icing (confectioners') sugar

Apple on a bed of nuts

This nut purée is even more delicious if the nuts are roasted and peeled at home before grinding them. It is ideal on a cold winter's day, accompanied by a punch or served as a pudding with vanilla ice cream.

4 Bramley or other tart apples

juice of 1 lemon

4 eggs

160 g/5½ oz (scant ¾ cup) sugar

1 vanilla pod

2 tablespoons rum

60 g/2 oz (½ cup) ground walnuts

60 g/2 oz (½ cup) ground hazelnuts

60 g/2 oz (½ cup) ground almonds

50 g/2 oz (4 tablespoons) melted butter

4 tablespoons red currant jelly

2 tablespoons flaked (slivered) almond

❶ Peel the apples and remove the core with an apple corer. Roll immediately in lemon juice to prevent it from going brown.

❷ Separate the eggs. Beat the egg yolks with sugar until very foamy. Cut the vanilla pods lengthways and remove the pulp. Stir into the egg mixture together with the rum. Then add the ground nuts and almonds to this mixture.

❸ Beat the egg whites until stiff and carefully fold into the egg yolk mixture with a spatula.

❹ Butter four ramekins and fill with the nut mixture. Put an apple in each one and fill the hole left by the core with a spoonful of red currant jelly. Spread the rest of the butter on each apple and sprinkle with flaked (slivered) almonds.

❺ Preheat the oven to 200°C (400°F), Gas mark 6 and bake on the middle shelf for about 35 minutes.

Serves 4. About 790 kcal per serving.

Viennese apple gratin

The apples dissolve into a delicate compote under the light, airy topping.
Raisins soaked in rum or blackberries may be added to the apples. The dish is
delicious served with vanilla ice cream.

1 Peel the apples, cut into quarters, remove the core and cut into thin slices.
Bring to the boil in the apple juice or wine, sweetened with brown sugar, and
simmer over low heat for about 5 minutes.

2 Fry the almond flakes in a pan without fat until golden yellow.

3 Separate the eggs, beat the egg yolks with 30 g/1 oz (2 tablespoons) sugar
until they become pale yellow. Beat the egg whites until stiff with the rest of
the sugar and add to the egg yolk mixture. Sieve the flour and baking powder
over this mixture and fold gently into the egg yolk mixture using a spatula.

4 Put the apple slices in a greased gratin dish and sprinkle with the roast
almond flakes. Pour the egg mixture on top and sprinkle with cinnamon sugar.

5 Preheat the oven to 200°C (400°F), Gas mark 6 and bake on the middle
shelf for about 20 minutes.

Serves 4. About 455 kcal per serving.

4 Bramley or other tart apples

juice of 1 lemon

**100 ml/3½ fl oz (½ cup) apple
juice or white wine**

60 g/2 oz (¼ cup) brown sugar

**2 tablespoons flaked (slivered)
almonds**

4 eggs

60 g/2 oz (¼ cup) sugar

100 g/3½ oz (1 cup) flour

½ teaspoon baking powder

2 tablespoons cinnamon sugar

icing (confectioners') sugar

Orange soufflé

The fruit acids and slight bitterness of the orange zest makes this a very refreshing pudding. Time can be saved by preparing the cooked egg sauce in advance. The oven must not be opened to check on the soufflé or it will almost certainly collapse.

3 untreated oranges

10 tablespoons orange liqueur

300 ml/10 fl oz (1¼ cups) milk

25 g/1 oz (4 tablespoons) flour

30 g/1 oz (2 tablespoons) sugar

40 g/1½ oz (3 tablespoons) butter

4 eggs

1 tablespoon icing (confectioners') sugar

❶ Wash the oranges in hot water and wipe dry. Grate the zest of 1 orange. Separate all the oranges into segments and cut into thin slices. Pour 5 tablespoons of orange liqueur over them and put in a cool place.

❷ Pour 3 tablespoons of milk over the flour and stir to a smooth mixture. Bring the rest of the milk to the boil. Stir in the flour and milk mixture and bring back to the boil. Stir in 30 g/1 oz (2 tablespoons) butter cut into small pieces. Separate the eggs, whisk in the egg yolks over low heat and continue stirring until the sauce thickens, but do not let it to boil. Stir in the rest of the orange liqueur and leave to cool.

❸ Butter a round, oven-proof gratin dish with the rest of the butter and sprinkle with icing (confectioners') sugar.

❹ Beat the egg whites until stiff and carefully fold into the egg sauce. Spoon into the gratin dish, preheat the oven to 180°C (350°F), Gas mark 4 and cook on the middle shelf for about 30 minutes. Serve with the orange fillets.

Serves 4. About 420 kcal per serving.

Nectarine gratin with coconut macaroons

The coconut macaroons give this dish a distinctive aroma. Instead of nectarines, you can also use plums or apricots. The macaroons can be replaced by plaited bubs or white bread. It is delicious served with vanilla ice-cream or vanilla sauce.

1 Peel the nectarines (it is helpful to blanch them briefly in boiling water first), cut into half, remove the stone and cut into slices. Wash the red currants and strip the currants from the stalks.

2 Mix the cinnamon with 100 g/3 1/2 oz (1/2 cup) sugar. Generously butter a gratin dish and arrange alternate layers of macaroon and nectarine slices mixed with red currants. Sprinkle each layer of fruit with cinnamon sugar.

3 Separate the eggs and beat the egg yolks with the rest of the sugar until foamy. Stir in the milk and thickening agent. Beat the egg whites very stiff and carefully fold into the egg yolk mixture with a spatula.

4 Spoon the egg and milk mixture over the alternate layers of fruit and macaroons and sprinkle with flaked (slivered) almonds. Preheat the oven to 180°C (350°F), Gas mark 4 and bake on the middle shelf for about 40 minutes.

Serves 4. About 690 kcal per serving.

6 nectarines

250 g/9 oz red currants

175 g/6 oz (¾ cup) sugar

1 tablespoon cinnamon

250 g/9 oz coconut macaroons

3 eggs

125 ml/4 fl oz (½ cup) milk

15 g (½ oz) thickening agent

3 tablespoons flaked (slivered) almonds

butter for the dish

Pumpkin gratin with pears

This dish is quite time-consuming to make but definitely worth it. It can be served as a sweet main dish accompanied by a zabaglione. It may also be made without sugar and served with fried meat.

1 To make the yeast dough, pour the flour in a bowl and make a well in the centre. Warm the milk with 2 teaspoons of sugar and crumble the fresh yeast into it. Pour the milk and yeast into the well and stir a little flour into it. Cover and leave to rest for about 15 minutes in a warm place. Add knobs of butter along the edge and work into a dough. Cover and leave to rest again, this time for about 30 minutes.

2 Peel the pumpkin, remove the seeds and cut the flesh into cubes. Cook the diced pumpkin until tender in a little water with the lid on and drain. Purée the pumpkin with a potato masher and season with cinnamon and nutmeg. Wash the lemon in hot water, wipe dry, grate the zest thinly and squeeze the juice. Add the juice and zest to the pumpkin mixture. Separate the eggs and stir the egg yolks into the pumpkin mixture.

3 Peel the pears, cut into quarters, remove the core and cut into thin slices. butter a gratin dish and arrange the pear slices in it.

4 Knead the dough again, roll out to the right size and put on top of the pear slices.

5 Beat the egg whites until stiff with the rest of the sugar . Carefully fold into the pumpkin mixture and spread on the dough. Dot the remaining butter in knobs over the surface of the dough , preheat the oven to 200°C (400°F), Gas mark 6 and cook on the middle shelf for about 50 minutes.

Serves 6. About 580 kcal per serving.

250 g/9 oz (2½ cups) flour

150 ml/5 fl oz (⅝ cup) milk

150 g/5 oz (½ cup) sugar

15 g/½ oz fresh yeast or 1 7 g/¼ oz packet powdered yeast

30 g/1 oz (2 tablespoons) soft butter

2 kg/4½ lb pumpkin

½ teaspoons cinnamon

freshly ground nutmeg

zest and juice of 1 untreated lemon

3 eggs

50 g/2 oz (4 tablespoons) butter

1 kg/2¼ lb pears

Baked fruit salad with caramel

This is a very popular pudding in Italy. The fruit can be varied according to the season. Stone-fruits and dried fruit are perfect for this dish but currants and berries produce too much juice. It is delicious served with ice cream or whipped cream.

1 Soak the dried fruit overnight in lukewarm water. Drain and cut the larger fruit into pieces.

2 Wash the apples and pears, peel, remove the core and cut into eight segments. Wash the oranges in hot water, wipe dry and grate the zest. Peel the oranges and lemon, remove the white pith and cut the fruit diagonally into thin slices.

3 Grease a gratin dish and line the bottom with half the apple and pear slices. Cover with half the dried fruit mixture and arrange the orange and lemon slices on top. Arrange the other half of the apple and pear slices on top. Peel the bananas, cut into slices, place over the lemon and orange slices and arrange the rest of the dried fruit on top.

4 Sprinkle with almond flakes and sugar. Mix the wine and grated orange zest and pour over the fruit. Preheat the oven to 220°C (425°F), Gas mark 7 and cook on the middle shelf for about 30 minutes.

5 Remove the fruit from the oven. Make the caramel sauce with 4 tablespoons of the cooking juice and brown sugar and pour over the fruit. Serve lukewarm or cold.

Serves 4. About 585 kcal per serving.

3 tablespoons raisins

3 dried figs

6 dried dates

6 dried prunes

6 dried apricots

2 sharp apples

2 pears

2 untreated oranges

1 lemon

1 banana

50 g/2 oz (⅜ cup) flaked (slivered) almond

5 tablespoons sugar

600 ml/20 fl oz (2½ cups) red wine

6 tablespoons brown sugar

Bread pudding with currants

The brown bread and egg-based sauce combines beautifully with the tartness of the red currants. It is also very useful that it can be prepared in advance. The pudding is equally delicious made with blueberries or cranberries. Serve cold with whipped cream.

500 g/18 oz red currants

3 eggs

125 g/4 oz (½ cup) sugar

1 packet vanilla sugar

1 pinch cardamon

1 pinch cinnamon

zest of 1 untreated lemon

1 tablespoon butter

75 g/3 oz dark bitter chocolate

500 g/18 oz black bread or pumpernickel

❶ Wash the red currants and strip from the stalks.

❷ Separate the eggs. Beat the egg yolks, vanilla sugar and sugar with a hand-held-whisk until the mixture begins to thicken and turns pale yellow. Stir in the cardamom, cinnamon and lemon zest.

❸ Butter a gratin dish. Grate the chocolate into thin shavings.

❹ Make the breadcrumbs in a liquidizer or food processor and stir into the egg yolk mixture. Beat the egg whites until stiff and carefully fold into the egg yolk mixture using a spatula.

❺ Put half the red currants into the gratin dish, cover with half the egg-based sauce and sprinkle with chocolate shavings. Pour the rest of the red currants over all and cover with the remaining sauce. Cover with aluminium foil.

❻ Preheat the oven to 180°C (350°F), Gas mark 4 and cook on the middle shelf for about 45 minutes

Serves 4. About 665 kcal per serving.

Sweet bread gratin

Bread pudding that uses up stale bread is a very traditional dish, born of
necessity. It is transformed here into a fabulous sweet main course or rich
pudding by the addition of some delicious ingredients. Serve with whipped
cream, maple syrup and perhaps some fruit compote.

1 Pour the rum over the raisins and leave to soak for at least 1 hour.

2 Roast the flaked (slivered) almonds in a non-stick pan without any fat until
golden yellow.

3 Butter a gratin dish. Beat the eggs with sugar and butter until very foamy
and add the cinnamon, lemon zest, apple juice and cream.

4 Cut the plaited bun into thin slices and arrange in the gratin dish so that
they overlap. Sprinkle the raisins and almonds on top.

5 Pour the egg mixture over all, preheat the oven to 200°C (400°F), Gas mark
6 and bake on the middle shelf for about 25 minutes.

Serves 4. About 890 kcal per serving.

100 g/3½ oz (⅔ cup) raisins

3 tablespoons rum

100 g/3½ oz (¾ cup) flaked
(slivered) almonds

75 g/3 oz (5 tablespoons) soft
butter

4 eggs

100 g/3½ oz (½ cup) sugar

1 tablespoon cinnamon

zest of 1 untreated
lemon

125 ml/4 fl oz (½ cup) apple juice

125 ml/4 fl oz (½ cup) cream

400 g/14 oz plaited bun or other
bread

Sweet potato gratin

This inexpensive dish is quick and easy to make and can be served, for instance, with soured cream and cinnamon sugar or a fruit compote. You can also add raisins or other dried fruits to the sweet potatoes.

500 g/18 oz potatoes

4 eggs

150 g/6 oz (¾ cup) soft butter

150 g/5 oz (generous ½ cup) sugar

1 packet vanilla sugar

butter for the dish

❶ Peel the sweet potatoes, cut into pieces and cook until tender. Drain and push through the potato press while still hot.

❷ Separate the eggs. Whisk together the sugar, vanilla sugar and egg yolks until very foamy. Stir into the sweet potatoes.

❸ Beat the egg whites until stiff and carefully fold into the sweet potato mixture with a spatula.

❹ Spoon the sweet potato mixture into a buttered gratin dish and level off. Preheat the oven to 200°C (400°F), Gas mark 6 and cook on the middle shelf for about 40 minutes until golden brown.

Serves 4. About 640 kcal per serving.

Sweet rice gratin with fruit

This simple gratin can be prepared with any seasonal fruit, and in winter tinned fruit can be used. It is delicious served with a fruit or vanilla sauce. If the gratin is served cold, it can be cut like a cake.

1 Bring the milk to the boil with 20 g/¾ oz (1½ tablespoons) sugar, add the rice and simmer over a very low heat for about 20 minutes, stirring often. Leave to cool a little.

2 Wash the apricots, cut into half and stone. Toast the flaked (slivered) almonda in a pan without any fat until golden yellow.

3 Separate the eggs, beat the egg yolks with the rest of the sugar until very foamy and add together with the lemon zest to the rice. Stir in the toasted almonds.

4 Beat the egg whites until stiff and carefully fold into the rice mixture. Spoon this rice mixture into a buttered gratin dish, level off and press the apricot halves into the surface. Dot the rest of the butter in flakes over it.

5 Preheat the oven to 200°C (400°F), Gas mark 6 and cook on the middle shelf for about 40 minutes.

Serves 4. About 550 kcal per serving.

500 ml/17 fl oz (2¼ cups) milk

70 g/2½ oz (scant ⅓ cup) sugar sugar

125 g/5 oz (⅝ cup) pudding rice

500 g/18 oz apricots

50 g/2 oz (⅜ cup) flaked (slivered) almonds

3 eggs

zest of 1 untreated lemon

50 g/2 oz (4 tablespoons) soft butter

500 ml/17 fl oz (2¼ cups) milk

100 g/3½ oz (½ cup) sugar

125 g/5 oz (⅝ cup) pudding rice

30 g/1 oz (¼ cup) candied lemon peel

30 g/1 oz (¼ cup candied orange peel

100 g/3½ oz (1 cup) candied fruit

2 untreated oranges

4 eggs

grated zest of 1 untreated lemon

50 g/2 oz chopped (½ cup) pistachio nuts

butter for the dish

Rice gratin with candied fruit

This is a really mouth-watering delicacy and a wonderful pudding. Any candied fruit can be used as desired. It is excellent served hot or cold with a sour fruit compote or with fruits preserved in rum and sugar.

❶ Bring milk to the boil together with 25 g/1 oz (2 tablespoons) sugar, stir in the rice and simmer for about 20 minutes over a very low heat, stirring often. Allow to cool slightly.

❷ Finely dice the candied lemon peel, orange peel and candied fruit. Wash the oranges under hot water, dry them and grate the zest finely. Next peel the orange, remove the white pith and cut the oranges into slices.

❸ Beat the egg yolks with 50 g/2 oz (¼ cup) sugar until very foamy. Add to the rice together with the lemon zest. Next stir in the candied lemon-peel, candied orange peel, candied fruit, pistachio nuts and orange zest.

❹ Beat two egg whites until stiff and fold carefully into the mixture. Pour into a gratin dish and level off. Preheat the oven to 200°C (400°F), Gas mark 6 and cook on the middle shelf for about 35 minutes.

❺ Beat the other 2 egg whites until stiff and carefully add the rest of the sugar. Take the gratin out of the oven and arrange the orange slices on top. Cover with the stiffly beaten egg whites and make a few peaks with a spoon.

❻ Return to the oven but on the second shelf from the top and bake until the peaks in the meringue topping turn brown.

Serves 4. About 620 kcal per serving.

Rice gratin with meringue topping

750 ml/1¼ pints (3½ cups) milk

150 g/5 oz (⅔ cup) sugar

175 g/6 oz (¾ cup) pudding rice

50 g/2 oz (⅜ cup) flaked (slivered) almond

100 g/4 oz (½ cup) butter

4 eggs

zest of 1 untreated lemon

1 packet vanilla sugar

icing (confectioners') sugar

The meringue topping makes this gratin particularly irresitible. Serve with a tart fruit compote such as red currants or sour cherries. Adults would also enjoy it with ice-cold egg liqueur.

❶ Bring the milk to the boil with 35 g/11/4 oz (11/2 tablespoons) sugar sugar, add the rice and simmer over a very low heat for about 20 minutes, stirring often. Allow to cool a little.

❷ Roast the flaked (slivered) almonds in a pan without any fat until golden yellow. Butter a gratin dish.

❸ Separate the eggs, beat the egg yolks with the butter and half the sugar until very foamy and add to the rice mixture together with the lemon zest.

❹ Beat 1 egg white until stiff and fold carefully into the rice mixture. Spoon into the buttered gatin dish and level off.

❺ Beat the rest of the egg whites until stiff and carefully add the rest of the sugar. Cover the rice gratin with this meringue topping in a wavy pattern using a piping bag with a large nozzle.

❻ Sprinkle with the roast flaked (slivered) almonds. Preheat the oven to 180°C (350°F), Gas mark 4 and bake on the lowest shelf for about 35 minutes. Sprinkle with icing (confectioners') sugar just before serving.

Serves 4. About 780 kcal per serving.

Baked rice with mango

Mangoes vary enormously in quality so must be selected with care. For this dish ripe ones are esential. A mango's ripeness can be judged from its fragrance and by how soft it feels when pressed lightly with the finger. Thai mangoes are particularly aromatic.

1 Bring the milk to the boil with 75 g/2½ oz (⅜ cup) sugar, stir in the rice and simmer over a very low heat for about 20 minutes, stirring frequently. Leave to cool a little.

2 Peel the mangoes, cut in half, remove the stone and cut the flesh into small cubes. Purée half the diced mangoes. Wash the limes under hot water and dry. Grate the zest and squeeze the juice. Stir the lime juice and zest together with the rest of the sugar into the mango purée and put in the refrigerator.

3 Cut the crystallized ginger into thin strips and stir into the rice pudding together with the diced mango and quark.

4 Pour the rice pudding into a buttered gratin dish, level off and sprinkle with grated coconut and brown sugar. Preheat the oven the 200°C (400°F), Gas mark 6 and cook on the middle shelf for about 30 minutes.

5 Serve hot or cold with mango purée.

Serves 4. About 580 kcal per serving.

500 ml/17 fl oz (2¼ cups) milk

100 g/3½ oz (½ cup) sugar

125 g/5 oz (⅝ cup) pudding rice

2 mangoes

zest and juice of 1 untreated lime

2 tablespoons candied ginger

500 g/18 oz quark (20% fat)

50 g/2 oz (⅓ cup) grated coconut

2 tablespoons brown sugar

butter for the dish

Pineapple and rice gratin

The refreshingly acid flavour of pineapple contrasts pleasantly with the sweetness of the rice pudding. Try this gratin with other tart fruit, such as sour cherries.

500 ml/17 fl oz (2¼ cups) milk

1 pinch salt

125 g/5 oz (⅝ cup) pudding rice

1 pineapple

zest and juice of 1 untreated lime

2 eggs

100 g/3½ oz (½ cup) sugar

½ teaspoon cinnamon

2 tablespoons brown sugar

30 g/1 oz (2 tablespoons) butter

❶ Add a pinch of salt to milk and bring to the boil, next add in the rice and simmer over a very low heat, stirring often. Leave to cool a little.

❷ Peel the pineapple and remove the pointed brown parts. Cut the pineapple in half and remove the stalk. Cut one half into thin slices and the other into small cubes.

❸ Rinse the limes under hot water, wipe dry, grate the zest and squeeze the juice.

❹ Separate the eggs and beat the egg yolks with the sugar until the mixture becomes foamy. Add to the rice pudding together with the cinnamon, lime juice and zest and diced pineapple.

❺ Beat the egg whites until stiff and fold carefully into the rice mixture. Spoon into a buttered gratin dish, level off and garnish with the pineapple slices. Sprinkle with brown sugar and dot with a few knobs of butter. Preheat the oven to 200°C (400°F), Gas mark 6 and bake on the middle shelf for about 25 minutes.

Serves 4. About 445 kcal per serving.

Damson gratin

Use rather tart damsons for this gratin. This pudding is best eaten lukewarm with vanilla ice-cream or ice-cold vanilla sauce.

1 kg/2¼ lb damsons

300 g/10 oz (1⅓ cups) sugar

2 tablespoons fruit liqueur

100 g/4 oz (½ cup) soft butter

4 eggs

1 pinch salt

zest of 1 untreated lemon

250 g/9 oz (2½ cups) flour

2 level teaspoons baking powder

75 g/3 oz (½ cup) ground hazelnuts

icing (confectioners') sugar

❶ Wash the damsons, cut into quarters and stone them. Mix the damsons with 100 g/3½ oz (½ cup) sugar and the fruit liqueur and leave to soak.

❷ Butter a gratin dish.

❸ Beat the egg yolk with the butter, the rest of the sugar, salt and lemon zest until very foamy. Stir the baking powder into the flour, then sieve the flour into the egg mixture and stir.

❹ Beat the egg-whites until stiff and fold carefully into the egg yolk and flour mixture.

❺ Put half the dough in the gratin dish, arrange the damsons on top and cover with the rest of the dough. Sprinkle with the hazelnuts, Preheat the oven to 180°C (350°F), Gas mark 4 and bake on the middle shelf for about 1 hour. Sprinkle with icing (confectioners') sugar just before serving.

Serves 8. About 520 kcal per serving.

Fruit gratin

This gratin is extremely quick and easy to make. Use seasonal fruit or preserved fruit. It is delicious served with vanilla ice-cream or whipped cream.

1 Wash the fruit, prepare and cut into pieces or slices depending on the size of the fruit.

2 Separate the eggs. Make a smooth dough mixing together the egg yolks, milk and flour, using a hand mixer.

3 Beat the egg-whites until they form stiff peaks and gently add the sugar. Carefully fold the beaten egg-whites into the egg yolk mixture.

4 Butter the gratin dish, spoon in the dough and arrange the fruit and walnuts on top.

5 Preheat the oven to 200°C (400°F), Gas mark 6 and bake on the middle shelf for about 30 minutes.

Serves 8. About 510 kcal per serving.

250 g/9 oz mixed fruit
4 eggs
250 ml/8 fl oz (1 cup) milk
200 g/7 oz (2 cups) flour
50 g/2 oz (½ cup) shelled walnuts
75 g/2½ oz (⅓ cup) sugar
butter for the dish

Gratiné peaches

It is important to use ripe, fragrant peaches for this exquisite pudding. White peaches have a particularly intense aroma. Nectarines or apricots may also be used. Serve with vanilla or peach-flavoured ice cream.

4 large, ripe peaches

50 g/2 oz marzipan

1 egg

2 tablespoons Amaretto

100 ml/3½ fl oz (½ cup) crème fraiche

50 g/2 oz Amaretti (Italian macaroons)

2 tablespoons flaked (slivered) almond

❶ Peel the peaches. This is made easier by blanching them briefly in boiling water. Cut the peaches in half, remove the stone and arrange next to each other in a gratin dish with the cut surface upwards.

❷ Crumble the marzipan and work into a smooth paste with the egg and amaretto. Next stir in the crème fraîche.

❸ Crumble the Amaretti biscuits coarsely and fill the peach halves. Spread the creamy marzipan mixture over the fruit and sprinkle with flaked (slivered) almonds.

❹ Preheat the oven to 200°C (400°F), Gas mark 6 and cook on the second shelf from the top for about 25 minutes. Serve hot on separate plates with ice cream.

Serves 4. About 325 kcal per serving.

Baked brioche pudding

This is a sophisticated version of the traditional bread pudding. As an alternative, thick slices of plaited bun may be used.

1 Peel the apples, remove the cores with an apple corer and cut the apples into slices.

2 Melt the butter in a pan and butter a shallow gratin dish. Fry the apple slices briefly in the melted butter over low heat, then add the pear syrup, apple juice and lemon juice and simmer gently for about 5 minutes.

3 Whisk the eggs and cream vigorously and add the cinnamon, then add the apple juice mixture.

4 Cut the brioche into finger-thick slices and arrange in alternate layers with the apple slices so that they overlap, adding a spoonful of cranberries in the holes in the apple slices.

5 Pour the egg and cream mixture on top, preheat the oven to 180°C (350°F), Gas mark 4 and bake on the second shelf from the bottom for about 25 minutes. Sprinkle with icing (confectioners') sugar just before serving.

Serves 4. About 550 kcal per serving.

2 large, Bramley or other tart apples

40 g/1½ oz (3 tablespoons) butter

3 tablespoons pear syrup

125 ml/4 fl oz (½ cup) apple juice

juice of 1 lemon

3 eggs

1 tablespoon cinnamon

150 ml/5 fl oz (⅝ cup) cream

4 small brioches

4 tablespoons cranberry jelly

icing (confectioners') sugar

Cooking glossary

Glossary of technical and foreign language cooking terms

baking, roasting

Cooking food in the oven in a heat-resistant dish, in a baking tin (pan) or on a baking (cookie) sheet. The food is cooked by the hot air of a conventional or a fan oven (a fan oven the same cooking effect is achieved with a lower temperature; see the maker's manual). The temperature most commonly used is 180°C (350°F), Gas Mark 4, which is ideal for cakes, biscuits (cookies), tarts, flans, roasts, fish and poultry. For puff pastry, soufflés and gratins the temperature should be between 200°C (400°F), Gas mark 6 and 220°C (425°F), Gas mark 7. More delicate food such as fish, veal and some poultry may need a lower heat, from 150° C (300°F), Gas mark 2 to 160° C (325°F), Gas mark 3.

As a rule of thumb, the lower the temperature, the longer the cooking time.

bain-marie

A container of hot water in which or over which food is gently cooked. It may be a rectangular pan in which pans are placed, but in the domestic kitchen it usually takes the form of a double boiler, a saucepan with a smaller pan fitting over it. It can be improvised satisfactorily by using a bowl over a saucepan containing about 2.5 cm/1 inch of hot water.

A bain-marie is used when it is essential not to overheat what is being cooked. It is used for processes such as melting chocolate, and for cooking sauces or puddings containing cream or eggs. For instance, to make a chocolate mousse, the egg whites are beaten stiff over a warm bain-marie. This makes a particularly airy, light yet firm mousse. A bain-marie is also indispensable for making a successful Hollandaise or Béarnaise sauce. The egg yolks are slowly heated while being stirred until they reach the correct consistency, so that they combine with the melted butter whisked into it little by little.

barding

Covering very lean meat such as saddle of venison, pheasant or saddle of hare with slices of bacon, secured with kitchen string. This ensures that the meat remains juicy and does not dry out, while also adding a pleasant flavour to the meat.

basting

Spooning liquid over food while it is being roasted. Normally the cooking juices are used, but butter, wine, stock (broth) or plain water can be used as well. This constant basting and 'looking after' the meat ensures that it remains juicy and does not dry out. The basting liquid acquires a very intense flavour.

beurre manié

Kneaded butter, used to thicken casseroles and sauces. Equal amounts of flour and butter are kneaded together and added as small knobs into boiling liquid while stirring constantly. This thickening agent has a delicious buttery taste and it is easy to handle because the butter and flour are mixed before being adding to the liquid, reducing the risk of lumps forming in the course of cooking.

blanching

Cooking vegetables such as spinach, leeks and carrots briefly in fast-boiling water. It is important to refresh the vegetables by plunging them in ice-cold water immediately afterwards. This ensures that the vegetables remain crisp and retain their original colour. After blanching, the vegetables are heated in hot stock (broth) or butter before serving.

blini

Pancake (crepe) made of a Russian batter using buckwheat flour, fried in a special small frying pan (skillet) about 15 cm (6 in) in diameter. Wheat flour is often added to the buckwheat flour so that it binds more easily. Blinis are usually served with caviar. They are also delicious with braised meat and game.

boiling

Cooking in liquid that is boiling. The process is synonymous with the concept of cooking. The food is cooked in a large amount of water and the agitation of the liquid will prevent the ingredients sticking to each other. So long as the water is boiling, the temperature will be 100°C (212°F) for the whole of the cooking time.

bouquet garni

A small bundle of various fresh herbs (usually parsley, thyme and bay leaves), tied together and cooked with the food. The bouquet garni is removed before serving.

braising

This refers to a method of cooking which combines frying, simmering and steaming. First the food is seared in hot oil or fat on all sides. This seals the meat, forming a thin crust; this also forms roasting matter on the bottom of the pan which is very important for the colour and flavour of the sauce. Liquid is then added to the meat, the pan is sealed with a lid and the food is slowly braised in a preheated oven. The method is also good for vegetable and fish dishes. It is excellent for less tender, strongly flavoured cuts of meat such as oxtail, goulash, braising steak or stewing lamb.

breadcrumbs

Dried white crumbs, made from stale bread without the crust. They are used in stuffing mixtures or to coat fish, poultry or other meats such as lamb chops.

brunoise

Finely diced vegetables or potatoes.

canapé

Small, bite-sized pieces of bread with various toppings such as smoked salmon, foie gras, caviar, smoked duck breast, ham and so on. They are served as an appetizer.

carcass

The carcass of poultry used in the preparation of chicken stock (broth). Fish bones are used in a similar way to make fish stock (broth).

carving

Cutting meat or poultry into slices or small pieces for serving. It is a good idea to carve on a carving board with a groove for the juices, using a special carving knife.

casserole

A large heat-resistant cooking pot usually made of cast iron or earthenware, excellent for slow-cooked dishes braises and stews such as oxtail and game ragout. Because of the casserole's large surface area and the lengthy cooking time, the meat is able to release it full flavour. Casseroles may be round or oval, the latter shape being ideally suited for long-shaped pieces of meat such as leg of lamb, rolled cuts of meat or a chicken.

célestine

Fine strips of pancake (crepe) added to soup as a garnish.

chiffonade

Finely cut strips of lettuce, often served with shrimp cocktail.

chinois

Conical strainer or sieve used to strain sauces and soups.

clarification

The removal of cloudy matter from soups, stock (broth) or jelly with lightly beaten egg white. The egg white attracts all the foreign particles which cause the cloudiness and can then be easily removed. The operation is carried out as follows. A lightly beaten egg white is added to some lean minced (ground) beef and chopped vegetables and a few ice cubes are stirred in. The mixture is added to the stock (broth), which should also be well chilled. Heat up while stirring constantly. The egg white begins to thicken at 70°C (160°F) and in the process it attract all the impurities in

the stock (broth). The stock (broth) becomes clear while developing a very intense flavour, as a result of the beef and vegetables. Fish and vegetable stock (broth) can also be clarified in the same way; in these cases the meat is omitted.

coating

The operation of pouring sauce over vegetables, meat or fish.

It also describes the technique of covering slices of meat and fish with beaten egg and breadcrumbs before frying them in hot oil. This gives the food a crisp coating while keeping the inside moist and juicy.

concassée

Blanched, peeled, quartered and de-seeded tomatoes, finely chopped. The term may also be applied to herbs.

consommé

Simple soup made of meat or chicken stock (broth), sometimes garnished. When clarified, it is known as clear or 'double' consommé. Cold consommé is often a jelly.

cream soup, velouté soup

Cream soups are thickened with béchamel sauce. Velouté soups are thickened with an egg and cream mixture. The soup should not be brought back to the boil after the mixture has been added to because the egg yolk would curdle.

crêpes

Thin pancakes made from a batter consisting of milk, flour and eggs. The pancakes are cooked slowly in a frying pan (skillet) until golden. They can be served as a dessert, plain with a sprinkling of sugar and lemon juice, or spread or filled with jam or chocolate. They can also be served as a savoury dish, stuffed with vegetable or other fillings.

deep-frying

The process of cooking food by immersion in hot fat. When the food is cooked and crisp, it is removed from the fat or oil in its basket or with a skimming ladle and left to drain thoroughly on kitchen paper. Because hot oil or fat often spatters it is vital to be extremely careful and avoid the risk of fire. An electric chip pan with an adjustable thermostatically-controlled temperature control is an excellent idea not only because it is safer but it also creates much less of a smell. Peeled potatoes cut into chips (sticks) or slices, shrimps and vegetables in batter are ideal for deep-frying, while deep-fried semolina dumplings are delicious served in soup. Deep-frying is also used for sweet dishes such as doughnuts and apple fritters.

duxelles

Garnish or stuffing consisting of finely chopped mushrooms sweated with diced onions and herbs.

forcemeat or stuffing

Finely chopped meat or fish used to stuff eggs, meat, pasta and so on. It can make a dish in its own right, as in the case of meat balls and quenelles, for example. It is also used as a basis for terrines and pâtés such as deer terrine or wild boar pâté.

filleting

The operation of cutting off the undercut of beef sirloin or similar cuts of pork (tenderloin), veal or lamb; removing the breasts of poultry from the carcass; or cutting the flesh of fish in strip-like pieces from the backbone.

flamber

Pouring spirits (such as brandy, rum or Grand Marnier) over food and setting light to it. The process is used with both savoury and sweet dishes, such as Crêpes Suzette. The spirits need to be warmed slightly first.

fleurons

Small pieces of puff pastry baked into various shapes such as flowers, little ships or shrimps. They are served with fish dishes in a sauce or with chicken fricassée.

flouring

The coating of pieces of fish or meat with flour before frying. This forms a tasty crust round the meat or fish which will be particularly juicy as a result.

frying

Frying is the process of cooking food in hot fat. The best fats and oils for frying are therefore ones that can be heated to a high temperatures such as sunflower oil, clarified butter or goose fat. When butter is used, a little oil is often added to raise the temperature it will reach without burning. Some cuts of meat such as beef steaks or pork cutlets may be fried in a non-stick griddle pan without any fat.

gazpacho

Cold Spanish vegetable soup made with fresh tomatoes, cucumbers, garlic and fresh herbs. It is particularly delicious on a hot summer's day.

glazing

Creating a glossy surface on vegetables, meat, fish or puddings. A suitable stock (broth), the cooking juices, a light caramel, jelly, hot jam or icing is poured over the food in question.

gnocchi

Small dumplings, originally Italian, made from potato, semolina or bread flour, depending on the region, poached briefly in boiling water.

gratiné

Baking dishes under a very high top heat until a brown crust has formed. The ideal topping is grated cheese, breadcrumbs or a mixture of the two.

grilling (broiling)

Cooking with intense radiant heat, provided by gas, electricity or charcoal, the latter giving the food a particularly delicious flavour. The food is cooked on a grid without fat, and grilling (broiling) is therefore particularly good for people who are calorie conscious. Meat, fish, poultry and even vegetables can be cooked in this way.

healthy eating

A well-balanced, varied diet based on wholesome, nutritious foods in the right proportion. Ingredients recommended include wholemeal (wholewheat) products, organic meat, fish and poultry and fresh fruit and vegetables.

julienne

Peeled vegetables cut into thin sticks, the length and thickness of matchsticks. They are cooked in butter or blanched and used as a garnish for soup, fish, meat or poultry dishes.

jus

The name given to cooking juices produced during roasting. It is also to describe brown stock (broth) prepared from various kinds of meat.

kaltschale

Literally 'cold cup', this is a cold sweet soup made with fruit and wine. The fruit, for instance raspberries, melon and strawberries, is finely puréed with lemon juice and wine if so desired to which fresh herbs are added. It is important that it is served chilled.

larding needle

Special needle for pulling lardons (strips of pork fat) through lean meat to keep it moist and make it more tender.

marinade

A mixture based on vinegar, lemon juice, buttermilk or yoghurt, with onions and other vegetables, spices and herbs. Meat or fish is steeped in the mixture for several hours to make it tender and enhance its flavour. Marinades can be also used for dressing salads or for marinating meat that is already tender. Meat marinades give sauces a particularly delicious flavour because they have absorbed the various flavours from the herbs, vegetables and spices.

marinating

Steeping meat or fish in a liquid containing salt, wine, vinegar, lemon juice or milk, and flavourings such as herbs and spices. Marinating has a tenderizing effect on the food and also improves the flavour because of the various ingredients added to the marinade. In addition, marinating also has a preserving effect on meat or fish so that it keeps longer. For instance, raw salmon may be marinated in salt, sugar, herbs and spices.

minestrone

Classic Italian vegetable soup using a wide variety of vegetables, the selection depending on the region and the season. However, pasta and beans are essential ingredients.

mirepoix

Finely diced vegetables, often with the addition of bacon and herbs, fried in butter and used as basis for sauces.

muffins

Round, flat rolls made with yeast dough and baked. In America, muffins are sweet rolls using baking powder as a raising agent, made in special muffin pans. There are many varieties, made for instance with blueberries, raspberries, red currants or chocolate.

pie

A sweet or savoury dish baked in a pastry shell with a pastry top. It is made in a pie tin (pan) with a slanting edge 5 cm (2 in) high. The lid of dough should have a small opening in the middle so that the steam can escape, preventing the inside from becoming distended.

ramekin or cocotte

A small, round oven-proof china or earthenware dish in which individual portions are cooked and served.

reducing

Concentrating a liquid by boiling it so that the volume is reduced by evaporation. It increases the flavour of what is left. Strongly reducing a

sauce gives a particularly tasty result with a beautiful shine.

refreshing

Dipping food, particularly vegetables, briefly in cold water after cooking to preserve the colour, mineral content and vitamins. The cooked vegetables or other items are then drained in a colander.

roasting

See baking.

roux

A mixture of butter and flour used to thicken sauces. The mixture is made by melting butter and stirring in flour. This is then diluted with milk or stock (broth) and cooked for at least 15 minutes while stirring constantly. For a dark roux, the flour is cooked until it turns brown before liquid is added. Because this reduces the thickening quality of the flour, the amount of flour should be increased.

royale

A custard-like cooked egg garnish. Milk and eggs are stirred together, seasoned, poured into small buttered moulds and poached in a bain-marie at 70–80°C (160–180°F). They are then turned out and diced.

salamander

Electric appliance used to caramelize or brown the top of certain dishes. It is comparable to a grill, which is normally used as a substitute.

sauté

Cooking food in fat in a frying pan (skillet). Small, uniform pieces of meat, fish, chopped vegetables or sliced potatoes are cooked in a pan while being tossed to prevent them sticking. In this way all sides of the food are cooked.

simmering

Cooked food in liquid over a low heat, just below boiling point. This method of cooking is often used for making soups and sauces since it makes the food tender and enables it to develop its full aroma..

soufflé

Particularly light, aerated dish made with beaten egg white which may be sweet or savoury. A meal which finishes with a mouth-watering chocolate soufflé will always be remembered with great pleasure.

soup bones

Meat bones, poultry carcass or fish bones used in making stock (broth). These are very important ingredients because they give an intense flavour to the stock (broth). Smooth beef and veal bones are ideal, but the marrow bone has the most flavour. It is important that the bones should purchased from a reliable butcher and come from a guaranteed source so as to avoid any risk of BSE (mad cow disease).

steaming

Cooking over a boiling water so that the food is out of contact with the liquid and cooks in the steam. To achieve this, the food is cooked in a perforated container over lightly boiling water or stock (broth). This method of cooking ensures that vegetables keep their flavour particularly well. They remain crisp and full of taste. Fish too can be cooked in this way without any addition-al fat but simply with herbs and spices. Steaming is particularly good for the preparation of low-calorie dishes for people who must follow a low-fat diet for reasons of health. But it will also appeal to everyone who loves the pure, genuine flavour of food.

stock (broth)

The flavoured liquid base of soups and sauces. Basic meat stocks (broths) for soups and sauces are made by simmering meat and bones of veal, beef, game, poultry or fish for several hours. As the liquid simmers gently, the constantly forming foam is periodically removed with a skimming ladle. When the stock (broth) has cooled down, the layer of fat can be removed so that the stock (broth) becomes light and clear. Vegetable stock (broth) is made in a similar way by boiling vegetables and herbs

straining

Filtering solid matter from liquids or draining liquids from raw or cooked food. Soups, sauces and stock (broth) are poured or pressed through a fine sieve. In the case of a stock (broth) the sieve may be lined with a coarse cloth.

string

Kitchen string is used to truss poultry or to tie a joint of meat so that it keeps its shape while being cooked.

suprême

Breast of chicken or game. The name refers to the best part of the bird, which is always prepared with the greatest care.

sweating

Frying the food lightly in a little fat in a pan over

moderate heat, so that it softens but does not brown.

tartlet

Small tart made from short crust or puff pastry with a sweet or savoury filling.

tenderizing

Making tough meat tender by beating it. The meat is placed between two sheets of foil and beaten with a mallet or the bottom of a small pan until it has become thin. It is used for roulades, veal escalopes and so on.

thickening

The addition of a substance to a sauce or soup to thicken it. There are several common methods. Flour may be added and stirred continuously until the liquid thickens. A variation is to mix butter and flour as a roux to which the liquid is slowly added, again stirring constantly. Alternatively egg yolk or cream can be stirred into the liquid to make an emulsion. On no account must it be allowed to boil or it will curdle. After the yolk has been stirred into the sauce or soup, it must not be cooked any more or it will curdle.

timbale

Mould lined with pastry, blind-baked and filled with meat, fish or other ingredients in a sauce, baked in the oven or cooked in a bain-marie.

trimming

The removal of connective tissue and fat from all kind of meats. The off-cuts are used in the preparation of stock (broth) and sauces. It is important to use a very sharp knife, held flat against the meat so as not to remove too much meat in the process.

turning

Forming vegetables and potatoes into decorative shapes, such as balls, ovals or spirals. This is carried out using a small knife with a crescent-shaped blade.

zest

The thin outer rind of oranges or lemons, used for its flavour and fragrance. It is cut from the pith in thin strips, using a zester.

Herbs and spices

agar

Thickening agent made from dried algae from Asia. It is used as a vegetable gelling agent, for instance in the manufacturing of blancmange powder, jelly or processed cheese. Agar only dissolves in very hot liquid and has highly gelatinous properties. It is therefore important to follow the instructions very carefully. It is particularly useful in vegetarian cuisine where it is an alternative to gelatine, which is made from beef bones. Agar is often combined with other thickening agents such as carob bean flour because it is very indigestible. This makes it a much more effective thickening agent.

allspice

These brown berries are grown in tropical countries, particularly Jamaica. The complex, multi-layered aroma of allspice is at its best when the fresh grains are crushed in a mortar. It is used to season lamb and beef ragouts, sausages, pies and gingerbread.

aniseed

Aniseed is often associated with the delicious aroma of Christmas cakes and pastries. The seed can be used whole, crushed or ground. It is also used in savoury dishes, for instance in the seasoning and marinades of fish and preparation of fish stock (broth). It is the main flavour of alcoholic drinks such as pastis and ouzo.

basil

Basil is undoubtedly the king of all fresh herbs used in the kitchen. It is an aromatic annual herb that plays an important part in a wide variety of dishes. It has a particular affinity with tomatoes and it is used in salads and many Mediterranean dishes.

basil, Thai

Thai basil is an important herb in Thai cuisine, used in baked noodle dishes, sauces and curries. It is available in many shops specialising in eastern food. It is very delicate and should be used as fresh as possible.

bay leaves

The leathery leaves of the bay tree have a spicy, bitter taste which becomes even stronger when dried. It is one of the ingredients of a bouquet garni. The fresh leaves are added to fish, while dried it is an important ingredient of many preserved dishes, such as braised meat marinated in vinegar and herbs, or pickled gherkins.

borage

A herb with hairy leaves and wonderful blue flowers. It has a slightly bitter, tangy taste reminiscent of cucumber and is mainly used in drinks such as Pimms. It is also a good accompaniment to salads, soups, cabbage and meat dishes.

burnet, salad

The leaves must be harvested before the plant flowers. Salad burnet is used in the same way as borage. It is only used fresh since it loses its aroma completely when dried.

caraway

Caraway is the traditional spice used in rich, fatty dishes such as roast pork, sauerkraut, raw cabbage dishes and stews – not simply for its aromatic flavour but also because of its digestive properties. It is added to some cheeses. Whole or ground, it is also used in spiced bread and cakes. Many liqueurs contain caraway because of its digestive properties.

cardamom

After saffron, cardamom is one of the most expensive spices in the world. Removed from the pod, the seeds are used ground. Just a pinch will be enough to add a delicious taste to rice dishes, cakes or gingerbread.

chervil

The fine flavour of chervil will enhance any spring or summer dish. It can be used in salads, soups and fish dishes and it is also very decorative.

chilli peppers

Red or green chilli peppers are hot and add a spicy, aromatic pungency to food. They are available fresh, dried, ground, pickled or in the form of a paste or essence (extract). When using fresh peppers, it is advisable to remove the seeds which are the hottest part. They are especially popular in Central and south-western America, the West Indies and Asia, forming an integral part of many dishes originating in these regions.

chives

This is one of the great traditional cooking herbs which is available throughout the year. Very versatile, chives are sold fresh in bunches and are delicious with fromage frais, bread and butter, scrambled eggs or fresh asparagus. The beautiful blue flowers of the chive plant are very decorative and also delicious, making a great addition with the leaves to any salad in the summer.

cloves

The flower buds of the clove tree have an intensely spicy aroma with a bitter, woody taste. That is why it should be used sparingly. Cloves are used in marinades, red cabbage and braised dishes as well as in mulled wine and many Christmas cakes and buns.

coriander (cilantro)

Coriander seeds have been used for a long time, mainly as a pickling spice and in Oriental dishes. Fresh green coriander leaves (cilantro) have become available in many countries much more recently. Finely chopped, this sweetish spicy herb adds an exotic aroma to many dishes, including guacamole. It should be used with discretion by those who are not used to the taste.

cress

The small-leafed relative of the watercress is slightly less aromatic. It is usually sold as small plants in paper containers or as seeds to grow oneself, often with mustard as the mustard and cress used in elegant sandwiches. Cress is commonly used to garnish egg dishes and salads.

cumin

This classic spice is common in eastern cuisine and is a fundamental ingredient of curry powder and curry pastes. It adds an interesting, exotic flavour to braised dishes such as lamb, kid or beef.

curry powder

Curry powder may be made from as many as 30 spices, including among others turmeric, pepper, cumin, caraway, cloves, ginger and allspice. It is extremely versatile and in addition to its use in curries it can be used in small quantities to add flavour to many meat, fish and poultry dishes.

dill

An annual sweetish aromatic herb, common in northern European cooking but seldom used in Mediterranean dishes. The feathery leaves are used fresh in fish dishes, sauces, with fromage frais, and in vegetable dishes. Cucumber pickles (dill pickles) make use of the leaves and the seeds.

fennel

Fennel leaves have a slight flavour of aniseed and are commonly used with fish. The seeds are sometimes used to season bread. When added to fish dishes and fish stock (broth), the seeds are crushed first.

fines herbes

Classic French combination of herbs, made from parsley, tarragon, chervil, chives, and perhaps thyme, rosemary and other herbs. Fines herbes may be used fresh, dried or frozen. The commonest use is in omelettes.

galangal

A close relative of the ginger family which is much used in south-eastern cuisine. The roots can used fresh, dried, ground or dried.

garam masala

The meaning of this Indian name is 'hot mixture', and it consists of up to 13 spices. It plays an important part in the cooking of India, where it is home-made, so that its composition varies from family to family. Garam masala is available commercially in supermarkets and in shops specialising in Asian food.

garlic

Cooking without garlic is unimaginable to anyone who loves and enjoys the pleasures of the Mediterranean. Freshly chopped, it enhances salads and cold sauces, roasts, stews, braised and grilled (broiled) dishes all benefit from the addition of garlic. Another popular use is in garlic bread.

gelatine

Gelatine is a thickening agent made from beef bones. Leaf gelatine must be soaked thoroughly in plenty of cold water for five or ten minutes before using it. It is then squeezed well and diluted in warm water. A special technique is needed when using gelatine in cream-based dishes. A few spoonfuls of cream are stirred into the gelatine. This mixture is then stirred into the rest of the cream. In this way lumps will be avoided.

ginger

The juicy roots of ginger have a sharp fruity aroma. Ginger adds an interesting, exotic touch to both savoury and sweet dishes. Because ginger freezes very well it can be kept for a long time without losing any of its flavour. A piece can be broken off whenever it is needed.

lavender

The taste of lavender is bitter and spicy. It can be used as a seasoning for lamb-based dishes, meat and fish stews and salads. The flowers are particularly decorative.

lovage

Lovage has a celery-like taste and both the stems and the leaves can be used in soup, salads and sauces. The finely chopped leaves are sometimes added to bread dumplings, and to the stuffing for breast of veal to which it adds a particularly delicate flavour.

marjoram

Sweet marjoram is a popular herb with a distinctive aroma. It can be used either fresh and dried, but like almost all herbs it is best when it is fresh. Marjoram is delicious in potato soups and omelettes. Pot marjoram is a hardier form with a stronger flavour, so it is advisable not to use too much.

mint

Mint is delicious as mint tea and also in puddings such a mint ice cream, and in drinks. It is part of many soups, salads and meat dishes, and is often added to potatoes and peas. Mint sauce is served with lamb. Mint leaves are also often used as decoration.

mugwort

This is a variety of wormwood. It grows in the wild and the sprigs should be collected just before the plants flower. They can also be dried for later use. Mugwort is popular with roast goose and game.

mustard seeds

Mustard seeds are one of the most important ingredients in pickled vegetables such as gherkins, courgettes (zucchini), pumpkin, mixed pickles and pickled cocktail onions. They are often used too in braised beef, marinated in vinegar and herbs.

nasturtiums

Nasturtium flowers are very decorative and the leaves are delicious, their sharp, peppery taste adding a spicy touch to any salad.

nutmeg

Grated nutmeg is delicious in soups, stews, potato purée and cabbage. It is a also a traditional seasoning in Christmas cakes and confectionery. It tastes best when freshly grated.

oregano

Also known as wild marjoram, oregano is much used in Italian cuisine. It is essential in many dishes such as pizzas, pasta with tomato sauce and aubergine (egg plant) dishes. In the case of pizzas it is best to use dried oregano because the fresh leaves become brown in the very strong heat of the hot oven, thus losing much of their flavour.

parsley

The most popular of all herbs, two varieties are common, one with curly leaves and the other with smooth leaves. But it is not only the leaves that are used; the roots too are full of flavour and are delicious added to soups and sauces. Parsley has a deliciously fresh aroma and a strong taste. It is also extremely rich in vitamins and minerals, so it is an important herb for use in winter.

pepper

Black pepper and white pepper have different tastes as well as looking different. Black pepper is obtained by harvesting the unripe fruit, while white pepper is the ripe fruit which is peeled before being dried. White pepper is milder, more delicate in taste and not as sharp as black.

purslane

The green, fleshy leaves can be used raw in salads or used as a vegetable in its own right as in the Far East. The delicious leaves have a slightly salty flavour.

rosemary

Rosemary has a particular affinity with lamb, which is often roasted with a few sprigs. It is particularly popular in France where it is used in many dishes such as soups, potatoes, vegetables, meat and fish dishes. Dried, chopped rosemary is one of the ingredients of herbes de Provence.

saffron

This bright orange spice is the 'golden' condiment of good cuisine, providing an inimitable flavour and colour. It consists of the dried stigmas of the saffron crocus, and about 4,000 of these are needed for 25 g (1 oz), which accounts for its high cost. But only a small amounts is needed; just a few filaments or a tiny pinch of ground saffron will be enough to add a very special taste to bouillabaisse, paella or risotto.

sage

The sharp, slightly bitter taste of sage is ideal with roast goose or roast lamb. Often used in sausages, it is also one of the most important ingredients of the Italian classic 'Saltimbocca' (veal escalope with sage and Parma ham). The fresh leaves are delicious dipped in batter and fried.

savory

Savory is a peppery herb used in many bean-based dishes and also in stews and casseroles. The stem is cooked in the stew while the young shoots are chopped up and added to the dish just before the end of the cooking time.

star anise

This is the small star-shaped seed of the Chinese aniseed, native to China. The flavour is a little more bitter than aniseed itself. It can be used for baking and cooking and adds a delicious flavour

to leg of lamb and dried apricots or in sweet and sour beef stew. It can also be used in puddings such as apple or quince compote.

tamarind

The pods contains a very sour juice which is much used in Indian and Thai cooking. Dishes such as baked fish with tamarind sauce, cherry tomatoes and fresh ginger are quite delicious.

tarragon

Tarragon has a delicate, spicy flavour. It can be used on its own as in tarragon vinegar or tarragon mustard, in Béarnaise as well as in a wide range of poultry and fish dishes. It is also excellent when combined with other herbs such as chervil, chives and parsley. The variety to be used is French tarragon. Russian tarragon grows easily from seed but has little flavour.

thyme

Like rosemary, this sweetish spicy herb is particularly good with Mediterranean food. It is an essential part of a bouquet garni and one of the main ingredients of herbes de Provence. Thyme will add a special touch to any dish, whether meat, fish, poultry or vegetables.

turmeric

Turmeric is much used in oriental cuisine. It is one of the basic ingredients of curry powder, Thai fish and meat curries and Indian rice dishes. It has an intense, yellow colour, but it should not be confused with saffron which has a very different taste.

vanilla

The fruit pods (beans) of the tropical vanilla orchid tree add a delicious aroma to cakes, puddings, ice cream, confectionery and so on. In cakes it is best to use vanilla essence (extract) while to make ice-cream and rice pudding, the crushed pod (bean) is added to the hot liquid so that it releases its delicate aroma. Vanilla sugar is made by leaving a pod (bean) in a container of sugar.

wasabi

Very sharp green radish usually available as a paste or powder. It used to season sushi and many other Japanese dishes. It is important not to add too much. Wasabi is usually served separately as well so that every one can mix it to the sharpness they like.

watercress

Watercress grows in the wild but it should not be eaten in case it contains paraites. Cultivated watercress is readily available. This is grown in watercress beds with pure water of the correct temperature running through them. Watercress has a hot, spicy taste and is delicious on its own, on bread and butter, in green salads, in cream soups, in risottos and in potato salad.

woodruff, sweet

Smelling of new-mown hay, sweet woodruff is only available in May, and it is therefore best-known as the essential ingredient in the aromatic drinks of traditional Maytime celebrations, such as the May wine cup in Germany and May wine punch in the United States. It is delicious in desserts, such as fresh strawberries marinated in woodruff, or wine jelly with fruit and fresh woodruff.

Index

Alphabetical list of recipes

List of recipes by category

Baked meat dishes

Baked fish dishes

Concept and execution: twinbooks, Munich
Editorial: twinbooks, Munich (Margit Hoffmann, Susanne Rieder, Dagmar Fronius-Gaier, Simone Steger, Sonya Mayer)
Layout and typesetting: twinbooks, Munich (Hubert Grafik Design, Munich)
English translation and typesetting: Rosetta International, London
Photography: twinbooks, Munich (Christian Kargl, Brigitte Sporrer, Alena Hrbkova)
Food styling: twinbooks, Munich (Tim Landsberg)
© Cover photograph: StockFood
Printing: Appl, Wemding

© 2001 DuMont Buchverlag, Köln (DuMont monte UK, London)
All rights reserved

ISBN 3-7701-7076-8

Printed in Germany

Author:
Conny Strauß is a freelance journalist and cook. After training in a hotel in Berlin, she now lives and works in Freiburg im Breisgau.

Photographers:
Christian Kargl acquired his interest in cooking from working as assistant to a food photographer. He works mainly in his own studio in Munich.

Brigitte Sporrer and Alena Hrbkova met each other while training as photographers in Munich, Germany. After working as assistants to various advertising and food photographers, they now each have their own studios in Munich and Prague respectively.

Food stylist:
Tim Landsberg, trained cook from Bonn, works in Munich as a freelance food stylist for clients including print and television advertising companies. He also works on cookery books.